Cheese and Eggs

Marshall Cavendish London & New York

Edited by Isabel Moore

Published by
Marshall Cavendish Publications Limited
58 Old Compton Street
London W1V 5PA

© Marshall Cavendish Limited 1973, 1974,
1975, 1976

This material first published by
Marshall Cavendish Limited in the
partwork *Supercook*

This volume first published 1976

Printed by Henri Proost, Turnhout, Belgium

ISBN 0 85685 167 1

Contents

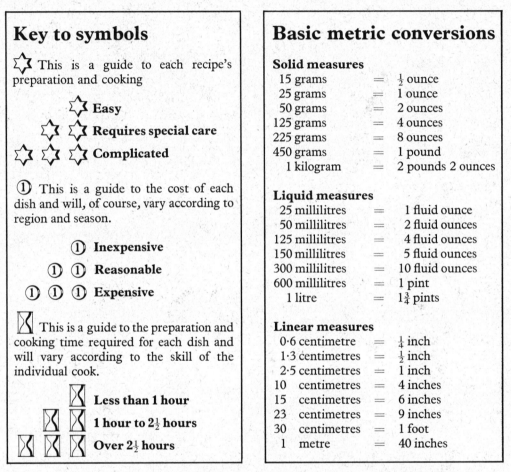

Key to symbols

☆ This is a guide to each recipe's preparation and cooking

　　　☆ **Easy**

　　☆ ☆ **Requires special care**

☆ ☆ ☆ **Complicated**

① This is a guide to the cost of each dish and will, of course, vary according to region and season.

　　① **Inexpensive**

　① ① **Reasonable**

① ① ① **Expensive**

⧖ This is a guide to the preparation and cooking time required for each dish and will vary according to the skill of the individual cook.

　　⧖ **Less than 1 hour**

　⧖ ⧖ **1 hour to $2\frac{1}{2}$ hours**

⧖ ⧖ ⧖ **Over $2\frac{1}{2}$ hours**

Basic metric conversions

Solid measures

15 grams	=	$\frac{1}{2}$ ounce
25 grams	=	1 ounce
50 grams	=	2 ounces
125 grams	=	4 ounces
225 grams	=	8 ounces
450 grams	=	1 pound
1 kilogram	=	2 pounds 2 ounces

Liquid measures

25 millilitres	=	1 fluid ounce
50 millilitres	=	2 fluid ounces
125 millilitres	=	4 fluid ounces
150 millilitres	=	5 fluid ounces
300 millilitres	=	10 fluid ounces
600 millilitres	=	1 pint
1 litre	=	$1\frac{3}{4}$ pints

Linear measures

0·6 centimetre	=	$\frac{1}{4}$ inch
1·3 centimetres	=	$\frac{1}{2}$ inch
2·5 centimetres	=	1 inch
10 centimetres	=	4 inches
15 centimetres	=	6 inches
23 centimetres	=	9 inches
30 centimetres	=	1 foot
1 metre	=	40 inches

American equivalents of food and measurements are shown in brackets.

Cheese and eggs

Eggs and cheese were, until recently, thought of primarily as 'fillers' — in the case of eggs, the perfect thing to go to work on, for cheese, a great thing for a snack with beer. Few people thought of them as a possible basis for dishes in their own right, so that it's only now that their true versatility is becoming apparent.

For if it's diversity you want, from casual nibbles to sumptuous desserts or cakes, then eggs and cheese are for you. You can catch up on a fabulous selection of basic (and not-so-basic) omelets and soufflés; or if it's inexpensive nourishing snacks that take your fancy, well, there are whole pages crammed full of mouth-watering rarebits and scrambles.

And you needn't restrict eggs and cheese to those end-of-the-week suppers for the family — they can be festive too, and there are whole sections in the book to prove it. If you need convincing, a quick glance at Cheese Fondue (pictured above, page 50) or Eggs Benedict (page 21) should do the trick; elegant dishes, both, guaranteed to make your dinner party swing.

For whatever the occasion, the recipes in this book will provide you with lots of easy-to-cook, practical dishes, at modest budget prices.

Eggs

Eggs have always been symbols of birth, rebirth, fertility and even witchcraft through the ages. Nowadays, however, they are chiefly valued as food in themselves and as an ingredient in cooking. Eggs are high in protein and fat, calcium, iron and vitamins.

Eggs should be eaten as fresh as possible; if you must store eggs, store them in a cool, airy place. If you store them in the refrigerator, allow them to warm to room temperature before using. To test the freshness of an egg, lay it, horizontally, in a bowl of cold water. If it stays horizontal it is fresh, but if it stands vertical it is too stale to eat.

PREPARING EGGS

Separating eggs: To separate eggs, crack them sharply then open them carefully just enough to let the white slip out. Tip the yolk carefully from one half of the shell to the other to let out all the white.

Beating egg whites: Whichever type of bowl you use, it must be without a trace of grease. To ensure this, rub the inside of the bowl with a piece of lemon.

Begin by beating slowly. When the whites begin to foam, add a pinch of salt (if you are using a stainless steel bowl add a pinch of cream of tartar instead) and quicken the pace of beating gradually until you are beating vigorously and the whites resemble stiff snow.

Beaten egg whites will not remain firm for long unless sugar has been added, and even then it will be for a short time only.

COOKING EGGS

In cooking, eggs may be prepared in many ways. The basic methods are: boiling, scrambling, frying, poaching and baking. Eggs can also be made into omelets or soufflés.

Boiled eggs: Boiled eggs should not, in fact, be boiled, but simmered gently to prevent them from cracking. There are two chief ways of soft boiling.

1. Place the egg in a pan of boiling water. Boil for 1 minute. Turn off the heat, cover the pan and leave for 5 minutes. (This is also known as coddling.)

2. Place the egg in a pan of boiling water and simmer for 3 to 4 minutes according to the size of the egg. At the end of this time the egg white will be lightly set and the yolk runny.

For a hard-boiled egg, put the egg in a pan of boiling water and bring the water back to the boil. Cook over moderate heat for 10 minutes. With a slotted spoon, remove the egg from the pan and place it at once under cold running water to prevent the yolk from discolouring.

Scrambled eggs: In a small bowl, beat 2 eggs together with $\frac{1}{2}$ teaspoon of salt, $\frac{1}{4}$ teaspoon of black pepper and, if liked, 2 tablespoons of milk, cream or water, until the mixture is frothy. In a medium-sized saucepan, melt 1 tablespoon of butter over moderate heat. Pour the egg mixture into the pan and cook for 3 to 4 minutes, stirring constantly with a wooden spoon until it thickens. Remove the pan from the heat and continue stirring until the mixture is creamy. Serve at once.

Fried eggs: In a small frying-pan, heat 1 tablespoon of olive oil or butter or bacon fat over moderate heat. When the oil or fat is sizzling, break an egg carefully into the pan. Reduce the heat to low and cook gently, basting frequently with the hot fat, until the white is set and the yolk is firm. Remove the fried egg from the pan with a spatula or fish slice.

Poached eggs: Poached eggs may either be cooked in boiling water or steamed in a poaching pan.

For the first method, half-fill a small saucepan with water. Add $\frac{1}{2}$ teaspoon of salt and 1 teaspoon of vinegar. Place the pan over moderate heat and bring the water to the boil. Break an egg into a cup. When the water is boiling, carefully tip the egg into the centre of the bubbling water. Reduce the heat to moderately low and simmer gently for 3 minutes. Remove the egg with a slotted spoon.

To use an egg-poaching pan, half-fill the bottom of the pan with water. Place $\frac{1}{4}$ teaspoon of butter in the centre of each cup, unless you are using a non-stick pan. Place the pan, with the cups in place, over the heat. When the water boils, break the eggs into the cups. Cover

and simmer for 3 to 5 minutes or until the eggs are lightly set. Loosen the eggs with a knife and slide them out on to a plate.

Baked eggs: One of the oldest methods of cooking eggs, baked eggs are usually prepared in individual cocotte dishes, although several may be baked together in a small ovenproof dish. Place the dishes or dish on a baking sheet. Put $\frac{1}{2}$ teaspoon of butter in each dish and place the baking sheet in the oven preheated to fairly hot 400°F (Gas Mark 6, 200°C) for 2 minutes. Break an egg into each dish, season with a little salt and pepper and return the dishes to the oven. Bake for 4 to 5 minutes or until the eggs are lightly set. Serve at once.

Omelet: To make good omelets, you will require a special omelet pan. The pan should be thick with a good smooth surface and should never be used for cooking anything else.

Never make too large an omelet. The best size is with 4 eggs and the limit should be 6 eggs. A medium-sized pan, one with a base 7 inches in diameter, will do for the smaller omelet and a pan with a 9-inch base for the larger.

To make an omelet for 3 people, break 6 eggs into a bowl. Add $\frac{1}{4}$ teaspoon of salt and pepper (or more if you like) and 2 tablespoons of cold water. Beat well to mix with either a fork or a wire whisk.

Heat the pan over moderate heat for 10 seconds or until it is quite hot. Add $\frac{1}{2}$ tablespoon of butter and when the foam subsides, pour in the beaten eggs. Stir the eggs, then leave them for a few seconds until the bottom sets. Reduce the heat to low. Using a palette knife or spatula, lift the edge of the omelet and at the same time tilt the pan away from you so that the liquid egg escapes from the top and runs into the pan. Put the pan down flat again over the heat and leave until the omelet begins to set. Tilt the pan away from you again and, with the help of the palette knife, flip one half of the omelet over to make a semi-circle. Slide the omelet quickly on to a heated plate and serve it immediately.

Soufflé: To make a cheese soufflé for four people, first grease a medium-sized soufflé dish with butter. Sprinkle 4 tablespoons of grated cheese (preferably a hard cheese, such as Cheddar) around the inside of the dish and press it on to the bottom and sides.

In a large saucepan, melt 2 ounces [$\frac{1}{4}$ cup] of butter over moderate heat. With a wooden spoon, stir 4 tablespoons of flour into the butter and cook, stirring constantly, for 1 minute. Remove the pan from the heat and add 10 fluid ounces [1$\frac{1}{4}$ cups] of milk, stirring constantly. Return the pan to the heat and cook the mixture, stirring constantly, for 1 minute or until it is thick and smooth.

Remove the pan from the heat and add salt, pepper and spices to taste. Beat 5 egg yolks, one at a time, into the hot sauce. Set aside to cool slightly.

Meanwhile, in a mixing bowl, beat 6 egg whites with a wire whisk or rotary beater until they form stiff peaks.

Stir 4 ounces [1 cup] of grated cheese (again preferably a hard cheese, such as Cheddar) into the cooling egg yolk mixture. When the cheese is blended, using a metal spoon, spoon the egg whites on top of the yolk mixture, then quickly fold them in.

Spoon the mixture into the prepared soufflé dish and cook in a fairly hot oven 400°F (Gas Mark 6, 200°C) for 25 to 30 minutes or until the soufflé has risen and is golden brown on top, and a skewer inserted into the middle comes out clean.

Remove the soufflé from the oven and serve it immediately.

Eggs Baked with Chicken Livers and Mushrooms

☆ ① ⊹

This is a light, tasty and nourishing dish which may be served as a first course or, if the quantities are doubled, as a main dish.

4 SERVINGS

1 oz. [2 tablespoons] butter
1 onion, finely chopped
4 slices lean bacon, diced
8 oz. chicken livers, roughly chopped
4 oz. button mushrooms, wiped clean and halved
2 tablespoons tomato purée
½ teaspoon salt
¼ teaspoon black pepper
4 eggs
2 oz. [½ cup] Cheddar or Parmesan cheese, finely grated

Preheat the oven to fairly hot 375°F (Gas Mark 5, 190°C). Grease four ramekin dishes or small individual baking dishes with half the butter.

In a small frying-pan, melt the remaining butter over moderate heat. When the foam subsides, add the onion and bacon and fry them for 5 minutes. Add the chicken livers and mushrooms and fry for a further 5 minutes or until the livers are lightly browned, the bacon crisp and the onion and mushrooms cooked. Remove the pan from the heat and drain off the excess fat.

Stir in the tomato purée, salt and pepper.

Put equal amounts of the liver mixture into each dish. Break an egg on top and sprinkle the cheese on top of the eggs. Bake in the centre of the oven for 15 to 20 minutes, or until the eggs are set and the tops lightly browned. Remove the dishes from the oven and serve immediately.

Egg and Corn Savoury

☆ ① ⊹

This delicious dish is simple, cheap and quick to prepare. It makes a tasty supper served with brown bread and butter.

4 SERVINGS

1 oz. [2 tablespoons] butter
1 garlic clove, crushed
1 medium-sized onion, thinly sliced
4 slices of stale white bread, crusts removed, cut into small squares
10 oz. canned condensed celery soup
2 tablespoons tomato purée
12 oz. frozen sweetcorn, thawed
15 oz. canned celery hearts, drained
½ teaspoon salt
¼ teaspoon black pepper
1 teaspoon paprika
1 tablespoon Worcestershire sauce
6 eggs
4 tablespoons milk
⅛ teaspoon grated numtmeg

In a large saucepan, melt the butter over moderate heat. When the foam subsides, add the garlic, onion and bread squares to the pan. Cook the mixture, stirring occasionally, for 5 to 7 minutes, or until the onion is soft and translucent and the bread squares are crisp.

Stir in the soup, tomato purée, corn, celery hearts, salt, pepper, paprika and Worcestershire sauce. Reduce the heat to

Egg and Corn Savoury is marvellously easy to prepare - and even easier to eat!

low, and simmer, stirring constantly, for 15 minutes.

In a small mixing bowl, beat the eggs, milk and nutmeg together. Stir the mixture into the pan.

Simmer for a further 10 minutes, stirring constantly, or until the mixture is thick and creamy. Remove the pan from heat and turn the savoury into a warmed serving dish. Serve at once.

√Egg Croquettes

☆ ☆   ①   ⧗ ⧗

A tasty lunch or supper dish, Egg Croquettes are delicious with tomato sauce and thick slices of wholemeal bread.

2 SERVINGS

3 oz. [⅜ cup] butter
2 oz. [½ cup] flour
8 fl. oz. [1 cup] milk
½ teaspoon salt
¼ teaspoon cayenne pepper
2 hard-boiled eggs, finely chopped
1 egg yolk
2 oz. [½ cup] seasoned flour, made with 2 oz. [½ cup] flour, 1 teaspoon salt and ½ teaspoon black pepper
1 egg, lightly beaten
2 oz. [⅔ cup] dry breadcrumbs

In a small saucepan, melt 1 ounce [2 tablespoons] of the butter over moderate heat. Remove the pan from the heat and, with a wooden spoon, stir in the flour to make a smooth paste. Gradually add the milk, stirring constantly.

Return the pan to the heat. Add the salt and cayenne and cook, stirring constantly, for 2 to 3 minutes or until the mixture is very thick and smooth.

Remove the pan from the heat and stir in the chopped eggs and egg yolk.

Spoon the mixture into a shallow bowl and cover. Place the bowl in the refrigerator to chill for 1 hour.

With well-floured hands, shape the mixture into balls.

Place the seasoned flour, beaten egg and breadcrumbs on three separate plates. Roll the balls first in the seasoned flour, then in the beaten egg and finally in the breadcrumbs, coating them on all sides.

In a medium-sized frying-pan, melt the remaining butter over moderate heat. When the foam subsides, add the croquettes and fry, turning occasionally, for 5 minutes, or until they are golden brown.

With a slotted spoon, remove the croquettes from the pan and serve at once.

√Curried Eggs

☆   ①   ⧗

Curried Eggs are ideal for an impromptu supper since they are quick and easy to prepare and very economical.

2-3 SERVINGS

2 oz. [⅓ cup] raisins
2 oz. [¼ cup] butter
2 onions, finely chopped
1 garlic clove, crushed
1 small tart apple, cored and diced
2 tablespoons flour

A filling, spicy supper dish – that's Curried Eggs.

2 teaspoons curry powder
8 fl. oz. [1 cup] milk
2 fl. oz. double cream [¼ cup heavy cream]
½ teaspoon salt
¼ teaspoon black pepper
4 hard-boiled eggs, halved
3 tablespoons slivered almonds, toasted

Place the raisins in a small bowl and cover with boiling water. Soak them for 10 minutes, then drain. Set aside.

Meanwhile, in a medium-sized saucepan, melt the butter over moderate heat. When the foam subsides, add the onions, garlic and apple to the pan. Cook, stirring occasionally, for 7 minutes, or until the onions and apple are soft but not brown.

With a wooden spoon, stir the flour and curry powder into the pan. Cook, stirring, for 3 minutes.

Remove the pan from the heat and stir in the milk. Return the pan to the heat. Cook, stirring, for 3 to 4 minutes or until the sauce has thickened. Stir in the cream, salt and pepper.

Carefully fold the egg halves into the sauce. Simmer the sauce for 4 to 5 minutes, or until the eggs are thoroughly heated.

Remove the pan from the heat. Serve the curry at once on a bed of rice with the raisins and almonds sprinkled on top.

Eggs Flamenco

☆ ① ①   ⏳

A quite delicious way of serving eggs, Eggs Flamenco can be served as a first course, as a light snack lunch or, accompanied by lots of crusty bread, for a family supper.

4 SERVINGS

- 4 tablespoons olive oil
- 1 medium-sized onion, thinly sliced
- 2 garlic cloves, crushed
- 8 oz. lean bacon, diced
- 2 small red peppers, white pith removed, seeded and chopped
- 6 medium-sized tomatoes, blanched, peeled and finely sliced
- 4 oz. mushrooms, wiped clean and finely sliced
- ½ teaspoon salt
- ¼ teaspoon freshly ground black pepper
- ⅛ teaspoon cayenne pepper
- 1 tablespoon chopped fresh parsley
- 8 oz. canned sweetcorn, drained
- 4 large eggs

Preheat the oven to moderate 350°F (Gas

Eggs Flamenco is a tasty mixture of bacon, red peppers, tomatoes, mushrooms, sweetcorn and eggs.

Mark 4, 180°C).

In a large frying-pan, heat the oil over moderate heat. Add the onion and garlic and cook, stirring occasionally, for 5 to 7 minutes, or until the onion is soft and translucent but not brown. Add the bacon and the red peppers to the pan and fry, stirring, for 10 to 12 minutes or until the peppers are soft. Stir in the tomatoes, mushrooms, salt, pepper, cayenne and parsley and continue cooking for 5 minutes, or until the tomatoes begin to pulp. Stir in the sweetcorn and remove the frying-pan from the heat.

Pour the mixture into an ovenproof baking dish. Using the back of a spoon, make four small depressions in the vegetable mixture. Break an egg into each depression.

Place the dish in the centre of the oven and bake for 25 to 30 minutes or until the eggs have set. Serve hot.

✓ Egg Flan

☆ ①   ⏳ ⏳

A quick and nourishing supper dish, Egg Flan is a tasty way to use up leftover vegetables. It may be served either hot or cold, for lunch or supper.

4 SERVINGS

PASTRY
- 6 oz. [1½ cups] flour
- ⅛ teaspoon salt
- 1½ oz. [3 tablespoons] butter
- 1½ oz. [3 tablespoons] vegetable fat
- 1 to 2 tablespoons iced water

FILLING
- 1½ oz. [3 tablespoons] butter
- 1 medium-sized onion, finely chopped
- 2 tablespoons flour
- 10 fl. oz. [1¼ cups] milk
- 1 large potato, cooked and sliced
- 1 large carrot, scraped, cooked and diced
- 2 tablespoons cooked peas
- ½ teaspoon salt
- ¼ teaspoon white pepper
- 4 hard-boiled eggs, sliced

6

2 oz. [½ cup] Cheddar cheese, grated

To make the pastry, sift the flour and salt into a medium-sized mixing bowl. Add the butter and vegetable fat and cut them into small pieces with a table knife. With your fingertips, rub the fat into the flour until the mixture resembles fine breadcrumbs.

Add 1 tablespoon of iced water and, using the knife, mix it into the flour mixture. With your hands, mix and knead the dough until it is smooth. Add more water if the dough is too dry. Chill the dough in the refrigerator for 30 minutes.

Preheat the oven to fairly hot 400°F (Gas Mark 6, 200°C).

Roll out the dough to ¼-inch thick. Lift the dough on your rolling pin and lay it over an 8-inch flan or pie dish. Ease the dough into the dish and trim the edges with a knife. Cover the dough with aluminium foil and a layer of dried beans. Place the dish in the oven and bake the dough blind for 15 minutes. Remove the dish from the oven. Remove the aluminium foil and dried beans. Return to the oven for 10 minutes or until the pastry is golden brown.

To make the filling, in a small saucepan, melt the butter over moderate heat. When the foam subsides, add the onion and cook for 5 to 7 minutes, or until it is soft and translucent but not brown.

Remove the pan from the heat. With a wooden spoon, stir in the flour to make a smooth paste. Gradually add the milk,

stirring constantly.

Return the pan to the heat and, still stirring, bring the sauce to the boil. Simmer for 2 to 3 minutes or until the sauce is thick and smooth. Stir in the potato, carrot, peas, salt and pepper.

Preheat the grill [broiler] to high.

Line the bottom of the pastry case with the hard-boiled eggs. Pour the sauce over the eggs. Sprinkle the top with the grated cheese and place the flan under the grill [broiler]. Grill [broil] for 3 to 4 minutes, or until the top is lightly brown. Serve at once, if you wish to eat the flan hot. Otherwise, allow the flan to cool to room temperature and then chill it for 30 minutes before serving.

Egg Flip I

☆ ① ⧖

This non-alcoholic Egg Flip is an ideal way to start the day.

1 SERVING

1 egg
½ teaspoon castor sugar
5 fl. oz. [⅝ cup] orange juice

In a small bowl, lightly beat the egg and sugar together with a fork. Gradually beat in the orange juice.

Serve at once.

Serve Egg Flan, hot or cold, as a nutritious lunch or supper dish, accompanied by salad and bread.

Egg Flip II

☆ ① ① ⧖

This warming drink is an alcoholic version of the basic egg flip and is ideal for a quick pick-me-up or nightcap.

1 SERVING

1 egg yolk
1 teaspoon sugar
1 tablespoon brandy
10 fl. oz. [1¼ cups] hot milk
¼ teaspoon grated nutmeg

In a small bowl, lightly beat the egg yolk and sugar together with a fork. Gradually beat in the brandy and hot milk. Pour the flip into a tumbler. Sprinkle over the nutmeg and serve.

Eggs with Mushrooms

☆ ① ⧖

A delicious dish of poached eggs, baked with cream, cheese and mushrooms, Eggs with Mushrooms makes an excellent light snack or appetizer for a main meal.

4 SERVINGS

1 tablespoon plus ½ teaspoon butter
4 eggs, lightly poached
8 oz. mushrooms, wiped clean and sliced
½ teaspoon salt
¼ teaspoon freshly ground black pepper
⅛ teaspoon cayenne pepper
3 fl. oz. single cream [⅜ cup light cream]
1 tablespoon finely chopped fresh parsley
2 tablespoons grated Parmesan cheese

Preheat the oven to moderate 350°F (Gas Mark 4, 180°C).

With the ½ teaspoon of butter, grease a medium-sized baking dish. Arrange the poached eggs in the baking dish and set aside.

In a small saucepan, melt the remaining butter over moderate heat. When the foam subsides, add the mushrooms, salt, pepper and cayenne to the pan. Cook, stirring occasionally, for 4 to 5 minutes or until the mushrooms are cooked. Remove the pan from the heat.

Stir the cream into the saucepan, mixing well with the mushrooms and their juices. Stir in the parsley.

Pour the creamed mushrooms over the eggs. Sprinkle the grated Parmesan on top and bake at the top of the oven for 15 minutes, or until the cheese is lightly browned.

Remove from the oven and serve immediately.

Ranchers Eggs

☆ ① ⧖

A relatively inexpensive supper dish, Ranchers Eggs is delicious served with crusty French bread and butter.

6 SERVINGS

- 1 tablespoon olive oil
- 2 garlic cloves, crushed
- 2 onions, finely chopped
- 6 large tomatoes, peeled, seeded and chopped
- 2 oz. canned pimientos, chopped
- 1 green chilli, seeded and finely chopped
- 1 teaspoon sugar
- 1 teaspoon salt
- ½ teaspoon black pepper
- ½ teaspoon ground coriander
- 12 eggs
- 6 oz. [1½ cups] Cheddar cheese, grated
- 1 tablespoon butter, cut into small pieces
- ¼ teaspoon chilli powder

In a large frying-pan, heat the oil over moderate heat. Add the garlic and onions and fry, stirring occasionally, for 5 to 7 minutes, or until the onions are soft and translucent but not brown. Add the tomatoes, pimientos, chilli, sugar, salt, pepper and coriander to the pan.

Reduce the heat to low and simmer the mixture, stirring frequently, for 15 to 20 minutes or until it is soft and pulpy.

Preheat the oven to very hot 450°F (Gas Mark 8, 230°C).

Remove the pan from the heat and transfer the mixture to a large ovenproof baking dish. With the back of a tablespoon make 12 hollows in the mixture. Place one egg in each hollow. Sprinkle the cheese over the eggs. Dot the butter over the cheese and sprinkle on the chilli powder.

Place the dish in the centre of the oven and bake the eggs for 6 to 8 minutes or until the cheese is golden brown and the eggs have set. Remove the dish from the oven. Serve immediately.

✓ Scandinavian Bacon and Egg Cake

☆ ☆ ① ⧖

This traditional egg cake is cooked on top of the stove until it is set. Serve for brunch or a light supper.

Ranchers Eggs makes a spicy impromptu supper for the family. Serve with lots of crusty bread.

4 SERVINGS

- 8 oz. streaky bacon, sliced
- 6 eggs
- 4 fl. oz. double cream [½ cup heavy cream]
- 2 teaspoons flour
- ½ teaspoon salt
- ¼ teaspoon black pepper
- 2 tablespoons chopped chives

Cut each slice of bacon in half, crosswise. In a medium-sized frying-pan, fry the bacon over moderate heat for 4 to 6 minutes, or until it is golden brown.

With tongs, remove the bacon pieces from the pan and set them aside on kitchen paper towels to drain.

Pour out all but 1 tablespoon of bacon fat from the pan.

In a large mixing bowl, beat the eggs, cream, flour, salt and pepper together with a wire whisk.

Pour the egg mixture into the pan. Reduce the heat to very low.

As the mixture begins to set, lift the set edges to allow the liquid egg mixture to run on to the pan. Place the bacon on top and sprinkle over the chives. Cook for about 20 minutes, or until the underside is golden brown.

Slide the cake on to a warmed serving dish. Serve at once, cut into wedges.

Spanish-Style Eggs

☆ ① ⧖

Easy and quick to prepare, Spanish-Style Eggs is a tempting combination of green peppers, onions and tomatoes topped with fried eggs.

4 SERVINGS

3 tablespoons vegetable oil
2 medium-sized onions, sliced and pushed out into rings
1 garlic clove, chopped
2 small green peppers, white pith removed, seeded and sliced
6 tomatoes, blanched, peeled and sliced
4 black olives, stoned
½ teaspoon salt
¼ teaspoon black pepper
4 fried eggs, kept hot

In a medium-sized frying-pan, heat the oil over moderate heat. When the oil is hot, add the onions, garlic and green peppers. Cook, stirring frequently, for 5

Spanish-Style Eggs is fried eggs, served on a bed of tomatoes, onions, green peppers and black olives. Serve for a snack or supper, with lots of toast.

to 7 minutes or until the onions are soft and translucent but not brown.

Add the tomatoes, olives, salt and pepper and cook for a further 5 minutes, stirring frequently.

Remove the pan from the heat. Turn the mixture into a warmed serving dish and place the eggs on top.

Serve at once.

Eggs with Spinach

☆ ① ⧖

A classic dish, Eggs with Spinach is poached eggs on a bed of creamy spinach sauce. It makes a superb luncheon dish.

4 SERVINGS

12 fl. oz. [1½ cups] béchamel sauce
¼ teaspoon grated nutmeg
1½ lb. spinach, cooked, drained and puréed
8 poached eggs, kept warm
2 oz. [½ cup] Parmesan cheese, grated

In a medium-sized saucepan, combine one-quarter of the béchamel sauce with the nutmeg and spinach. Place the pan over moderate heat and cook, stirring constantly, for 3 to 4 minutes or until the sauce is hot and smooth.

Preheat the grill [broiler] to high.

Pour the spinach sauce into a medium-sized shallow flameproof serving dish. Place the poached eggs on top. Spoon the remaining béchamel sauce over the eggs, and sprinkle the top with the cheese. Place the dish under the grill [broiler] and grill [broil] for 3 to 4 minutes or until the top is brown and bubbly.

Remove the dish from the heat and serve immediately.

Cheese Omelet

One of the simplest of supper dishes, Cheese Omelet is also one of the tastiest and quickest to prepare. Serve with a tossed mixed green salad, sautéed potatoes and brown bread liberally spread with butter for a really satisfying informal meal.

2-3 SERVINGS

6 eggs
¼ teaspoon salt
¼ teaspoon freshly ground black pepper
2 tablespoons cold water
1 tablespoon butter
3 tablespoons grated cheese (either Parmesan or Cheddar or a mixture of Gruyère and Parmesan)

In a medium-sized mixing bowl, beat the eggs, salt, freshly ground pepper and water together with a kitchen fork until they are well mixed.

In a large omelet pan, melt the butter over moderate heat. When the foam subsides, pour in the egg mixture. Stir the eggs, then leave them for a few seconds until the bottom sets. Reduce the heat to low. Using a palette knife or spatula, lift the edges of the omelet and, at the same time, tilt the pan away from you so that the liquid egg escapes from the top and runs on to the pan. Put the pan down flat over the heat and sprinkle over the grated cheese. Leave until the omelet begins to set again. Tilt the pan away from you again and, with the help of the palette knife, flip one half of the omelet over to make a semi-circle.

Remove the pan from the heat and slide the omelet quickly on to a heated serving dish.

Cut into two or three and serve it at once.

Green Pea Omelet

A deliciously different omelet, Green Pea Omelet may be served with fried potatoes and buttered carrots.

2-3 SERVINGS

4 oz. peas, weighed after shelling
1¼ teaspoons salt
1 oz. [2 tablespoons] butter
6 eggs
¼ teaspoon freshly ground black pepper
2 tablespoons cold water

Place the peas in a medium-sized saucepan and sprinkle over 1 teaspoon of the salt. Add enough water just to cover the peas. Place the pan over moderately high heat and bring the water to the boil. Reduce the heat to moderate and cook the peas for 8 to 10 minutes or until they are tender.

Remove the pan from the heat and drain the peas in a colander.

Purée the peas in a food mill or in an electric blender. Place the purée in a small bowl. Add half of the butter and stir until the butter has melted. Set aside and keep warm.

In a medium-sized mixing bowl, beat the eggs, the remaining salt, the freshly ground pepper and water together with a kitchen fork until they are well mixed.

In a large omelet pan, melt the remaining butter over moderate heat. When the foam subsides, pour in the egg mixture. Stir the eggs, then leave them for a few seconds until the bottom sets. Reduce the heat to low. Using a palette knife or spatula, lift the edges of the omelet and, at the same time, tilt the pan away from you so that the liquid egg escapes from the top and runs on to the pan. Put the pan down flat over the heat and leave until the omelet begins to set again.

Spoon over the pea purée. Tilt the pan away from you again and, with the help of the palette knife, flip one half of the omelet over to make a semi-circle.

Remove the pan from the heat and slide the omelet quickly on to a warmed serving dish.

Cut into two or three and serve it at once.

Omelet with Haddock, Cream and Cheese

This omelet is different from the classic French omelet in that the eggs are separated and the omelet finished cooking under the grill [broiler]. Serve with puréed spinach for a light but satisfying meal.

2-3 SERVINGS

1½ oz. [3 tablespoons] butter
4 oz. cooked, flaked smoked haddock
5 fl. oz. double cream [⅝ cup heavy cream]
6 eggs, separated
3 tablespoons grated Parmesan cheese
½ teaspoon salt
¼ teaspoon black pepper
1 tablespoon chopped fresh parsley

In a small frying-pan, melt 1 ounce [2 tablespoons] of the butter over moderate heat. When the foam subsides, add the smoked haddock and 2 tablespoons of cream, stirring well to mix. When the cream is hot, remove the pan from the heat and set aside to cool.

In a large mixing bowl, beat the egg yolks with half of the cheese and the salt, pepper and parsley. Add the fish mixture.

In another large mixing bowl, beat the egg whites with a wire whisk or rotary beater until they form stiff peaks. With a metal spoon, fold the egg whites into the haddock mixture.

Preheat the grill [broiler] to high.

In a large omelet pan, melt the remaining butter over moderate heat. When the foam subsides, pour in the egg mixture.

Leave it for 2 minutes or until the bottom sets and becomes brown.

Sprinkle over the remaining cheese and pour over the remaining cream. Remove the pan from the heat and place it under the grill [broiler]. Grill [broil] for 30 seconds.

Remove the pan from the grill [broiler]

and transfer the omelet to a warmed serving dish. Cut into two or three and serve at once.

Ham Omelet

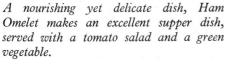

A nourishing yet delicate dish, Ham Omelet makes an excellent supper dish, served with a tomato salad and a green vegetable.

2-3 SERVINGS

1 oz. [2 tablespoons] butter
2 oz. lean cooked ham, diced
6 eggs
¼ teaspoon salt
¼ teaspoon black pepper
2 tablespoons cold water

In a small frying-pan, melt half of the butter over moderate heat. When the foam subsides, add the ham and cook, stirring occasionally, for 5 minutes or until the ham is heated through and very lightly browned. Remove the pan from the heat and set aside. Keep warm.

In a medium-sized mixing bowl, beat the eggs, salt, pepper and water together with a fork until they are well mixed.

In a large omelet pan, melt the remaining butter over moderate heat. When the foam subsides, pour in the egg mixture. Stir the eggs, then leave them for a few seconds until the bottom sets. Reduce the heat to low. Using a palette knife or spatula, lift the edges of the omelet and, at the same time, tilt the pan away from you so that the liquid egg escapes from the top and runs on to the pan. Put the pan down flat over the heat and leave until the omelet begins to set again. Spoon over the ham. Tilt the pan away from you again and, with the help of the palette knife, flip one half of the omelet over to make a semi-circle.

Remove the pan from the heat and slide the omelet quickly on to a warmed serving dish. Cut into two or three and serve at once.

Herb Omelet

One of the great classic French omelets, Herb Omelet makes a delicious and elegant lunch dish. Serve with buttered asparagus tips and a green salad and, to drink, a well-chilled white Chablis wine.

2-3 SERVINGS

6 eggs
¼ teaspoon salt
¼ teaspoon freshly ground black pepper
2 tablespoons cold water
1½ tablespoons chopped fresh mixed herbs
1 tablespoon butter

In a medium-sized mixing bowl, beat the eggs, salt, pepper, water and mixed herbs together with a fork until they are well mixed.

In a large omelet pan, melt the butter over moderate heat. When the foam subsides, pour in the egg mixture. Stir the eggs, then leave them for a few seconds until the bottom sets. Reduce the heat to low. Using a palette knife or spatula, lift the edges of the omelet and, at the same time, tilt the pan away from you so that the liquid egg escapes from the top and runs on to the pan. Put the pan down flat over the heat and leave until the omelet begins to set again. Tilt the pan away from you again and, with the help of the palette knife, flip one half of the omelet over to make a semi-circle.

Remove the pan from the heat and slide the omelet quickly on to a heated serving dish.

Cut into two or three and serve it at once.

Onion, Mushroom and Bacon Omelet

This sustaining dish may be served with grilled [broiled] tomatoes and a mixed salad, for supper or lunch.

2 SERVINGS

1 oz. [2 tablespoons] butter
1 medium-sized onion, finely chopped
2 lean bacon slices, rinds removed and diced
4 medium-sized mushrooms, wiped clean and thinly sliced
4 eggs
¼ teaspoon salt
¼ teaspoon freshly ground black pepper
1½ tablespoons cold water

In a small frying-pan, melt half of the butter over moderate heat. When the foam subsides, add the onion and bacon and cook, stirring occasionally, for 5 minutes. Add the mushrooms and cook for a further 3 minutes, or until the mushrooms are lightly cooked and the bacon is crisp. Remove the pan from the heat and, with a slotted spoon, transfer the mixture to a plate. Set aside and keep the mixture warm.

In a medium-sized mixing bowl, beat the eggs, salt, pepper and water together with a fork. Add the onion mixture and beat briskly until the ingredients are well mixed.

In a medium-sized omelet pan, melt the remaining butter over moderate heat. When the foam subsides, pour in the egg mixture. Stir the eggs, then leave them for a few seconds until the bottom sets. Reduce the heat to low. Using a palette knife or spatula, lift the edges of the omelet and, at the same time, tilt the pan away from you so that the liquid egg escapes from the top and runs on to the pan. Put the pan down flat over the heat and leave until the omelet begins to set again. Tilt the pan away from you again and, with the help of the palette knife, flip one half of the omelet over to make a semi-circle.

Remove the pan from the heat and slide the omelet quickly on to a warmed serving dish. Cut into two and serve at once.

13

Algerian Scrambled Eggs with Sausage and Green Peppers

☆ ① ① ⊠

This spicy dish is easy to prepare and can be served as a snack lunch or as an informal supper. Accompany with lots of crusty bread and lager.

4 SERVINGS

- ½ teaspoon cayenne pepper
- ¼ teaspoon ground cumin
- ⅛ teaspoon salt
- 2 tablespoons olive oil
- 1 lb. spicy sausage, such as hot Italian sausage or Spanish chorizos, cut into 1-inch rounds
- 1 garlic clove, crushed
- 14 oz. canned peeled Italian tomatoes, drained and chopped
- ¼ teaspoon freshly ground black pepper
- 2 medium-sized green peppers, white pith removed, seeded and cut into strips
- 6 eggs, lightly beaten

In a small dish, mix the cayenne, cumin and salt together. Set aside.

In a large, heavy frying-pan, heat the oil over moderate heat. When the oil is hot, add the sausage and fry, turning from time to time, for 4 minutes or until the slices are evenly browned and cooked through.

Stir in the garlic, cayenne mixture, the tomatoes and black pepper. Cook, stirring occasionally, for 3 minutes or until the mixture is thick. Add the pepper strips, cover and cook, stirring occasionally, for 8 minutes.

Pour the beaten eggs, a little at a time, over the sausage mixture, stirring constantly. Cook over low heat, stirring constantly, for 3 to 5 minutes or until the eggs are just scrambled.

Remove the pan from the heat, transfer the scrambled egg mixture to a warmed dish and serve at once.

✓Egg and Bacon Scramble

☆ ① ⊠

This tasty dish of eggs cooked with bacon and vegetables may be served as a light lunch or supper dish. Accompany with lots of hot buttered toast.

4 SERVINGS

- 1 tablespoon vegetable oil
- 1 medium-sized onion, finely chopped
- 8 slices streaky bacon,

Courgettes [zucchini], bacon, tomatoes, mushrooms and eggs form the basis of Egg and Bacon Scramble. It makes a filling, tasty and inexpensive dish.

coarsely chopped
- 4 courgettes [zucchini], trimmed and chopped
- 2 large tomatoes, blanched, peeled and chopped
- 4 oz. button mushrooms, wiped clean and halved
- ½ teaspoon salt
- ¼ teaspoon freshly ground black pepper
- 6 eggs
- 4 tablespoons milk
- ⅛ teaspoon grated nutmeg
- 2 oz. [1 cup] coarse fresh white breadcrumbs
- 1 tablespoon butter, cut into small pieces

In a shallow, flameproof casserole, heat the oil over moderate heat. When the oil is hot, add the onion and bacon and cook, stirring occasionally, for 7 minutes or until the onion is soft but not brown and the bacon pieces are cooked through and crisp.

Add the courgettes [zucchini], tomatoes, mushrooms, salt and pepper to the casserole. Reduce the heat to low and cook, stirring occasionally, for 15 minutes or until the courgettes [zucchini] are tender. Remove the casserole from the heat and set aside.

Preheat the grill [broiler] to moderately high.

In a medium-sized mixing bowl, beat

mixture. Cook for 5 to 7 minutes, stirring constantly, or until the eggs are firm and only slightly moist.

Remove the pan from the heat and transfer the mixture to a warmed serving dish.

Serve immediately.

Savoury Scramble

☆ ① ⧖

A delicious, spicy lunch or supper dish, Savoury Scramble is very quick to make and may be served on hot buttered toast.

4 SERVINGS

1 oz. [2 tablespoons] butter
1 medium-sized onion, finely chopped
10 lambs' kidneys, cleaned, prepared and quartered
2 oz. mushrooms, wiped clean and chopped
1 tablespoon flour
5 fl. oz. [⅝ cup] home-made beef stock
½ teaspoon Tabasco sauce
1 tablespoon tomato purée
2 tablespoons finely chopped fresh parsley
1 teaspoon salt
½ teaspoon freshly ground black pepper
8 eggs, lightly beaten

In a large saucepan, melt the butter over moderate heat. When the foam subsides, add the onion and fry, stirring occasionally, for 5 to 7 minutes or until it is soft and translucent but not brown. Add the kidneys and mushrooms and fry, stirring occasionally, for 3 minutes. Stir in the flour and cook for 1 minute. Remove the pan from the heat and gradually stir in the stock, Tabasco sauce and tomato purée. Return the pan to the heat and cook, stirring constantly, for 2 minutes. Reduce the heat to low and simmer for 20 minutes.

Stir in the parsley, salt and pepper. Remove the pan from the heat and stir in the eggs, beating with a wooden spoon until the ingredients are thoroughly combined. Return the pan to low heat. Stir for 3 to 5 minutes or until the eggs are set.

Remove the pan from the heat and serve at once.

---

the eggs, milk and nutmeg together. Stir the egg-and-milk mixture into the casserole. Return the casserole to the heat and cook gently, stirring constantly, until the eggs are nearly scrambled. Remove the casserole from the heat.

Sprinkle the breadcrumbs on top of the mixture and carefully dot with the butter pieces.

Place the casserole under the grill [broiler] and grill [broil] the mixture for 3 minutes or until the top is lightly browned.

Remove the casserole from the heat and serve immediately, straight from the casserole.

Matzo Brei

SCRAMBLED EGGS AND MATZO

☆ ① ⧖

A traditional Jewish breakfast dish served during Passover, Matzo Brei may also be served as an after-dinner savoury. Fried onions may be added if liked.

2 SERVINGS

2 matzos, broken into 2-inch pieces
4 fl. oz. [½ cup] milk
2 eggs, lightly beaten
½ teaspoon salt
⅛ teaspoon grated nutmeg
1 tablespoon butter

Place the matzo pieces in a large mixing bowl and pour over the milk.

Leave to soak for about 5 minutes. With a slotted spoon, transfer the matzos to a medium-sized mixing bowl. Discard any leftover milk.

Pour the eggs on to the matzos. Add the salt and nutmeg and mix well with a wooden spoon.

In a medium-sized saucepan, melt the butter over moderate heat. When the foam subsides, pour in the matzo and egg

15

Cheese and Sour Cream Soufflé

✓

☆☆   ①   ⊠

Adapted from an old Romanian recipe, Cheese and Sour Cream Soufflé may be served with salad as an unusual lunch or light supper dish.

4 SERVINGS

1 tablespoon butter, softened
3 teaspoons flour
8 oz. cream cheese
3 fl. oz. [⅜ cup] sour cream
3 egg yolks
3 fl. oz. [⅜ cup] milk
½ teaspoon salt
4 egg whites

Preheat the oven to fairly hot 400°F (Gas Mark 6, 200°C).

Using your fingertips or a piece of paper, spread the softened butter over the bottom and sides of a 7-inch soufflé dish. Sprinkle about 1 teaspoon of flour into the soufflé dish and shake it so that it evenly coats the insides. Knock out any excess flour and set the dish aside.

In a mixing bowl, beat the cream cheese with a wooden spoon until it is soft and creamy. Using a whisk, beat in the sour cream, a spoonful at a time. Continue to beat until the mixture is smooth.

Add the egg yolks, one at a time, beating well after each addition. Stir in the milk, salt and the remaining flour, beating briskly until the mixture is smooth.

In a large bowl, beat the egg whites with a wire whisk or rotary beater until they form stiff peaks. Using a metal spoon, fold the whites into the egg yolk and sour cream mixture.

Reduce the oven temperature to fairly hot 375°F (Gas Mark 5, 190°C) and pour the mixture into the prepared soufflé dish. Bake the soufflé in the centre of the oven for 25 to 35 minutes or until it has risen and is golden brown on top, and a skewer inserted into the middle comes out clean.

Remove the soufflé from the oven and serve immediately.

Parsnip Soufflé

☆☆   ①   ⊠

Parsnip Soufflé makes an unusual and deliciously flavoured lunch or supper dish.

Soufflés are relatively simple to make yet always seem somehow 'special' to eat - this Cheese and Sour Cream Soufflé is inexpensive enough to serve for a family supper, yet elegant enough for a party.

Serve with parsley potatoes and tomato salad.

4 SERVINGS

2 oz. [¼ cup] butter
3 medium-sized parsnips, peeled, cooked and drained
1 large onion, boiled, drained and chopped
½ teaspoon salt
1 teaspoon freshly ground black pepper
¼ teaspoon ground cloves
2 fl. oz. single cream [¼ cup light cream]
2 oz. [½ cup] flour
6 fl. oz. [¾ cup] milk
4 egg yolks
5 egg whites

Preheat the oven to fairly hot 400°F (Gas Mark 6, 200°C).

Using 1 tablespoon of the butter, grease a 3-pint [2-quart] soufflé dish and set it aside.

Using the back of a wooden spoon, rub the parsnips and onion through a large, fine strainer into a medium-sized mixing bowl. Add the salt, pepper and cloves and stir in the cream. Set aside.

In a medium-sized saucepan, melt the remaining butter over moderate heat. Remove the pan from the heat and, with the wooden spoon, stir in the flour to make a smooth paste. Gradually add the milk, stirring constantly.

Return the pan to the heat and cook, stirring constantly, for 2 to 3 minutes or until the sauce is thick and smooth. Add the parsnip mixture, stirring constantly, and continue cooking for a further 4 minutes.

Remove the pan from the heat and set aside to cool to lukewarm. Stir in the egg yolks and mix well until the ingredients are thoroughly combined.

In a medium-sized mixing bowl, beat the egg whites with a wire whisk or rotary beater until they form stiff peaks. Using a large metal spoon, carefully fold the egg whites into the sauce.

Pour the mixture into the prepared soufflé dish. Place the dish in the centre of the oven and reduce the heat to fairly hot 375°F (Gas Mark 5, 190°C). Bake for 20 to 30 minutes or until the soufflé has risen and is golden brown on top, and a skewer inserted into the centre comes out clean.

Remove the soufflé from the oven and serve immediately.

✓ Spinach Soufflé with Ham

☆☆   ①   ⊠

A tasty mixture of spinach, ham and cheese

combines to make Spinach Soufflé with Ham a satisfying dish to serve for a light lunch.

4 SERVINGS

3 oz. [⅜ cup] butter
2 shallots, finely chopped
4 oz. lean cooked ham, finely chopped
2 oz. [½ cup] flour
4 fl. oz. [½ cup] milk
4 tablespoons spinach purée
½ teaspoon salt
1 teaspoon freshly ground black pepper
1 teaspoon paprika
2 oz. [½ cup] Emmenthal cheese, grated
2 tablespoons single [light] cream
4 egg yolks
5 egg whites

Preheat the oven to fairly hot 400°F (Gas Mark 6, 200°C). Grease a 2½-pint [1½-quart] soufflé dish with a tablespoon of the butter. Set aside.

In a medium-sized saucepan, melt 1 ounce [2 tablespoons] of the remaining butter over moderate heat. When the foam subsides, add the shallots and ham and cook, stirring frequently, for 3 to 4 minutes or until the shallots are soft and translucent but not brown. With a slotted spoon, remove the shallots and ham from the pan and keep warm.

Add the remaining butter to the pan and melt it over moderate heat. Remove the pan from the heat and, with a wooden spoon, stir in the flour to make a smooth paste. Gradually add the milk, stirring constantly. Stir in the spinach.

Return the pan to the heat and cook, stirring constantly, for 2 to 3 minutes or until the sauce is thick and smooth. Stir in the salt, pepper, paprika and cheese and cook, stirring constantly, for a further 2 minutes or until the cheese has melted. Remove the pan from the heat and stir in the cream. Add the reserved shallot and ham mixture and stir well to mix. Set aside to cool to lukewarm, then beat in the egg yolks, one at a time.

In a mixing bowl, beat the egg whites with a wire whisk or rotary beater until they form stiff peaks. With a metal spoon, carefully fold the beaten egg whites into the sauce. Pour the mixture into the soufflé dish.

Place the dish in the centre of the oven and reduce the temperature to fairly hot 375°F (Gas Mark 5, 190°C). Bake for 25 to 30 minutes or until the soufflé has risen and is golden brown on top, and a skewer inserted into the centre comes out clean.

Remove from the oven and serve the soufflé immediately.

Eggs Stuffed with Ham and Herbs

Hard-boiled eggs stuffed with a delicious ham and herb mixture and then fried, Eggs Stuffed with Ham and Herbs may be served with a thick tomato and onion sauce for a superbly sustaining family lunch or supper.

2 SERVINGS

4 hard-boiled eggs
2 oz. cooked ham, very finely chopped
4 oz. [½ cup] butter
1 tablespoon finely chopped chives
2 teaspoons chopped fresh thyme or 1 teaspoon dried thyme
1 teaspoon Worcestershire sauce
2 eggs
½ teaspoon salt
¼ teaspoon freshly ground black pepper
4 tablespoons dry white breadcrumbs

Cut the eggs in half, lengthways. Remove the yolks and place them in a medium-sized mixing bowl. Set the whites aside. Add the ham, half of the butter, the chives, thyme, Worcestershire sauce, one egg, salt and pepper.

With a wooden spoon, cream the mixture thoroughly until it is well blended and smooth.

Spoon the mixture into the egg white halves. Sandwich the halves together to form a whole egg. The halves should not fit tightly together.

In a small bowl, lightly beat the second egg with a fork. Roll the stuffed eggs in the beaten egg and then in the breadcrumbs.

In a medium-sized frying-pan, melt the remaining butter over moderate heat. When the foam subsides, place the stuffed eggs in the pan and fry them, turning occasionally, for 5 minutes, or until they are golden brown all over.

With a slotted spoon, carefully transfer the stuffed eggs from the pan to a warmed serving dish.

Serve at once.

Mexican Stuffed Eggs

An unusual combination of egg, green pepper, avocado and prawns or shrimps, Mexican Stuffed Eggs may be served as a refreshing appetizer to dinner or as part of a cold buffet. Serve on a bed of lettuce leaves, garnished with sliced tomatoes and stuffed green olives.

6 SERVINGS

6 hard-boiled eggs
1 medium-sized avocado, peeled, stoned and chopped
1 medium-sized onion, finely minced
1 small green pepper, white pith removed, seeded and finely minced
4 oz. small prawns or shrimps, shelled, deveined and finely chopped
1 teaspoon lemon juice
1 teaspoon wine vinegar
½ teaspoon salt
½ teaspoon freshly ground black pepper
⅛ teaspoon cayenne pepper
1 tablespoon finely chopped fresh parsley

Slice the eggs in half, lengthways, and scoop out the yolks. Set the egg whites

Eggs Stuffed with Ham and Herbs are very versatile - serve them with tomato sauce, crusty bread and salad for a satisfying lunch or supper, or as a filling between-meals snack.

Mexican Stuffed Eggs are a spicy mixture of avocado, onion, green pepper and prawns or shrimps stuffed into hard-boiled egg halves.

aside. Using the back of a wooden spoon, rub the yolks and the avocado flesh through a fine nylon strainer into a medium-sized mixing bowl. Carefully stir in the onion, green pepper and chopped prawns or shrimps.

Add the lemon juice, vinegar, salt, pepper and cayenne, mixing well to blend. With a teaspoon, generously stuff the egg white halves with the mixture. Arrange the stuffed eggs on a serving dish. Sprinkle with the parsley and chill the eggs in the refrigerator for 30 minutes before serving.

✓ Scotch Eggs

☆ ☆   ① 　 ⧗

A very old favourite in the British Isles, Scotch Eggs are a delicious and nourishing snack or meal, with some tossed mixed salad and lots of liberally buttered brown bread. Served hot with a tomato sauce, or cold with a salad, they are ideal for the busy housewife to prepare. In past centuries, Scotch Eggs were sometimes called birds' nests.

4 SERVINGS

1 lb. pork sausage meat
2 teaspoons Worcestershire sauce
1 tablespoon seasoned flour, made with 1 tablespoon flour, ⅛ teaspoon salt, ⅛ teaspoon black pepper and ⅛ teaspoon dried thyme
4 medium-sized hard-boiled eggs
1 large egg, well beaten
2 oz. [⅔ cup] fine dry breadcrumbs sufficient vegetable oil for deep-frying

Place the sausage meat and Worcestershire sauce in a medium-sized mixing bowl. Add the seasoned flour mixture and blend the ingredients together with your hands. Divide the mixture into four equal pieces.

Mould each piece of meat around an egg and carefully roll each egg between your hands to shape the sausage meat coating.

Place the beaten egg and breadcrumbs in two separate, shallow dishes. Dip the eggs first in the beaten egg, and then in the breadcrumbs, coating them thoroughly and shaking off any excess crumbs. Set aside.

Fill a large saucepan or deep-frying pan one-third full with vegetable oil.

Place the pan over moderate heat and heat the oil until it reaches 350°F on a deep-fat thermometer or until a small cube of stale bread dropped into the oil turns light brown in 55 seconds.

Using tongs or a slotted spoon, carefully lower the eggs into the oil. Fry them for 5 minutes, or until they are deep golden brown.

Remove the pan from the heat. Using the tongs or slotted spoon, transfer the eggs to kitchen paper towels to drain.

Place the eggs on a warmed serving plate and serve at once, if they are to be eaten hot.

Eggs Stuffed with Tuna

☆ ☆   ① ①   ⧗ ⧗

Stuffed with a mixture of tuna fish, pickled gherkins and mayonnaise, these eggs make an attractive hors d'oeuvre or part of a cold buffet. Or serve them with lots of brown bread and butter for a light summer lunch or supper.

6-12 SERVINGS

2 oz. [¼ cup] butter
4 oz. canned tuna fish, drained and flaked
1 tablespoon lemon juice
4 tablespoons mayonnaise
¼ teaspoon freshly ground black pepper
½ teaspoon paprika
3 small, sweet pickled gherkins, finely chopped
12 hard-boiled eggs
1 bunch of watercress, washed and shaken dry

In a medium-sized mixing bowl, mash the butter and tuna fish together with a kitchen fork until they are thoroughly combined. Add the lemon juice, mayonnaise, black pepper, paprika and chopped pickled gherkins. Combine the ingredients thoroughly and set the bowl aside.

Cut off about 1 inch of the rounded end of each of the eggs. Retain these 'lids'. Slice a thin strip from the pointed ends of each of the eggs so that they will sit flat. Using a teaspoon, carefully remove the egg yolks from the whites, being careful to keep the whites intact. Set the whites aside.

Mash the egg yolks into the tuna fish mixture with a fork, mixing them in thoroughly. Carefully stuff the egg whites with the tuna and egg yolk mixture. Replace the 'lids' on top of the stuffed eggs.

Arrange the watercress on a large shallow serving dish. Place the eggs, standing upright, on the cress.

Place the serving dish in the refrigerator and allow the eggs to chill for 20 minutes before serving.

Eggs in Artichokes

☆ ☆ ① ① ⊠

These unusual stuffed artichokes make an ideal appetizer for a dinner or lunch party, being both decorative and delicious. They can also be served as a vegetable accompaniment to grilled [broiled] steak or chops.

4 SERVINGS

4 medium-sized artichokes, cooked and cooled
4 hard-boiled eggs
½ teaspoon salt
¼ teaspoon black pepper
⅛ teaspoon cayenne pepper
4 oz. canned sweetcorn, drained
2 tablespoons chopped fresh chives
2 tablespoons double [heavy] cream
1 oz. [2 tablespoons] butter, melted
3 oz. [¾ cup] Parmesan cheese, grated

Preheat the oven to moderate 350°F (Gas Mark 4, 180°C).

Gently pull the leaves of each artichoke apart and remove the yellow inner core. With a fork or spoon, scrape out the choke and discard it. Trim the base of each artichoke so that it stands upright. Place the artichokes in a baking dish.

Slice the eggs in half and scoop out the yolks. Rub the yolks through a fine strainer into a medium-sized mixing bowl. Finely chop the egg whites and add them to the bowl. Mix in the salt, pepper, cayenne, sweetcorn, chives and cream.

Fill the centre of each artichoke with the egg mixture. Using a pastry brush, coat the leaves of the artichoke with the melted butter. Top each filling with a liberal sprinkling of cheese.

Pour a little water around the artichokes and place the dish in the oven. Bake for 10 minutes or until the filling is melted and brown. Serve at once.

Eggs in Baked Potatoes

☆ ① ⊠ ⊠

A delicious and filling dish suitable for a light informal lunch or dinner, these baked potatoes are stuffed with a mixture of eggs, butter, cream and chives.

4 SERVINGS

4 large potatoes, scrubbed
1 tablespoon butter
1 tablespoon chopped chives
1 teaspoon salt
¼ teaspoon black pepper
⅛ teaspoon grated nutmeg
4 tablespoons double [heavy] cream
4 eggs

Preheat the oven to fairly hot 375°F (Gas Mark 5, 190°C).

Prick the potatoes lightly with a fork. Place the potatoes on the centre shelf in the oven and bake them for 1½ hours.

Remove the potatoes from the oven and cut off an inch from the top of each one. Scoop out the inside of each potato, taking care not to break the skin.

In a mixing bowl, mash the potato

Eggs in Baked Potatoes is a satisfying snack lunch.

flesh and butter together using a fork. Add the chives, salt, pepper and nutmeg. Stir in the cream and beat until the ingredients are thoroughly combined. Gradually beat in the eggs.

Stuff equal amounts of the egg and cream filling into each potato. Place the potatoes in a baking dish and return them to the oven. Bake for 10 to 12 minutes, or until the top of the filling is lightly browned. Serve immediately.

Eggs Benedict

☆ ☆ ① ① ⊠

Crumpets [English muffins] topped with ham, poached eggs and hollandaise sauce, Eggs Benedict is a famous American dish.

4 SERVINGS

8 thick slices cooked ham
8 crumpets [English muffins]
1 oz. [2 tablespoons] butter
8 hot poached eggs
HOLLANDAISE SAUCE
3 egg yolks
1 tablespoon cold water
4 oz. [½ cup] butter, softened
¼ teaspoon salt
⅛ teaspoon cayenne pepper
1 teaspoon lemon juice
1 tablespoon single [light] cream

Preheat the oven to very cool 275°F (Gas Mark 1, 140°C).

Preheat the grill [broiler] to high.

Place the ham slices on the grill [broiler] pan and grill [broil] them for 2 to 3 minutes on each side. Transfer the ham slices to an ovenproof dish and put it in the oven to keep warm.

To prepare the sauce, in a heatproof bowl set over a pan of hot water, beat the egg yolks and the water together with a wire whisk until the mixture is pale.

Gradually beat in the butter, in small pieces. Continue beating until the sauce begins to thicken.

Add the salt, cayenne and lemon juice. Beat in the cream. Remove the pan from the heat and set it aside. Keep warm.

Toast the crumpets [muffins] and spread them with the butter. Arrange the crumpets [muffins] on warmed plates. Place a slice of ham on each crumpet [muffin] and top with a poached egg.

Spoon a little of the sauce over each crumpet [muffin] and serve at once.

Egg Bread

☆ ① ⊠ ⊠ ⊠

This beautifully light Egg Bread, or Challah, is plaited [braided] and sprinkled with poppy seeds. It is traditionally baked

for Hebrew Sabbaths and festivals.

ONE 2-POUND LOAF

½ oz. fresh yeast
1½ tablespoons sugar
6 fl. oz. [¾ cup] milk, lukewarm
1 lb. [4 cups] flour
1½ teaspoons salt
2 eggs, beaten
1 tablespoon vegetable oil
½ teaspoon butter
GLAZE
1 egg yolk, beaten with 1 tablespoon cold water
2 tablespoons poppy seeds

Crumble the yeast into a small bowl and mash in ½ teaspoon of the sugar with a fork. Add 2 teaspoons of the warm milk and cream the milk and yeast together to form a smooth paste. Cover the bowl with a clean cloth and set it aside in a warm, draught-free place for 15 to 20 minutes, or until the yeast mixture has risen and is puffed up and frothy.

Sift the flour, remaining sugar and the salt into a large, warmed mixing bowl. Make a well in the centre of the flour and pour in the yeast mixture. Add the remaining milk, eggs and oil and, using a spatula, gradually draw the flour into the liquid. Continue mixing until all the flour is incorporated and the dough

Eggs Benedict, an American classic.

comes away from the sides of the bowl.

Cover the bowl with a clean damp cloth. Set the bowl in a warm, draught-free place and leave it for 1½ to 2 hours, or until the dough has risen and has almost doubled in bulk.

Grease a baking sheet with the butter.

Turn the risen dough out of the bowl on to a lightly floured surface and knead it for about 5 to 8 minutes. Divide the dough into three ropes, each about 12 inches long. Fasten the ropes together at one end and loosely plait [braid] the three pieces together, fastening again at the end.

Place the loaf on the greased baking sheet and cover it again with a clean cloth. Set it aside in a warm place for 2 to 2½ hours, or until the loaf has risen and expanded across the baking sheet.

Preheat the oven to hot 425°F (Gas Mark 7, 220°C).

Paint the top of the loaf with the egg yolk glaze and sprinkle the poppy seeds over the top. Place the baking sheet in the centre of the oven and bake for 10 minutes. Then reduce the temperature to fairly hot 375°F (Gas Mark 5, 190°C) and bake for a further 25 to 30 minutes or until the loaf is golden brown.

After removing the bread from the oven, tip the loaf off the baking sheet and rap the underside with your knuckles. If the bread sounds hollow, like a drum, it is cooked. If it does not sound hollow, return it to the oven for a further 5 to 10 minutes. Cool the loaf on a wire rack.

Eggs Caviar

☆ ① ①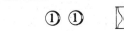

These stuffed eggs make an extravagant and tempting hors d'oeuvre.

6 SERVINGS

6 hard-boiled eggs
1 tablespoon black or red caviar
1 teaspoon lemon juice
¼ teaspoon cayenne pepper
1 bunch watercress

Cut the eggs in half, lengthways. Cut a thin slice off the bottom of each half so that the stuffed eggs will have a flat bottom. Remove the yolks and press them through a strainer into a bowl.

With a fork, beat the caviar, lemon juice and cayenne into the yolks.

Spoon the mixture into the egg whites. Arrange on a serving dish and chill for 30 minutes.

Garnish with the watercress and serve.

Egg-Drop Soup

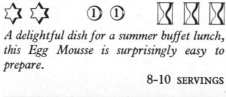

A light, delicate first course, this classic Egg-Drop Soup is adapted from a Cantonese recipe.

6 SERVINGS

1 tablespoon vegetable oil
1 medium-sized onion, thinly sliced
1 small cucumber, finely diced
3 pints [7½ cups] hot chicken stock
4 tomatoes, quartered
1 egg, lightly beaten

In a large saucepan, heat the oil over moderate heat. When it is hot, add the onion and cook, stirring constantly, for 1 minute. Add the cucumber to the pan and cook, still stirring, for 1 minute.

Stir in the chicken stock and bring it to the boil. Reduce the heat to low and simmer, stirring occasionally, for 10 minutes. Add the tomatoes to the soup and simmer for a further 5 minutes.

Remove the pan from the heat and beat the egg into the soup. Serve at once.

Eggs Mornay

Poached eggs and ham on toast with a creamy cheese sauce, Eggs Mornay is the ideal dish for a quick supper snack.

4 SERVINGS

4 slices hot, buttered toast
1 tablespoon butter
4 thick slices cooked lean ham
4 poached eggs, kept warm
SAUCE
1½ oz. [3 tablespoons] butter
3 tablespoons flour
8 fl. oz. [1 cup] milk
5 fl. oz. single cream [⅝ cup light cream]
½ teaspoon salt
¼ teaspoon black pepper
⅛ teaspoon cayenne pepper
1 teaspoon Worcestershire sauce
1 teaspoon paprika
2 oz. [½ cup] Cheddar cheese, grated

First make the sauce. In a saucepan, melt the butter over moderate heat. Remove the pan from the heat and, with a wooden spoon, stir in the flour to make a smooth paste. Gradually add the milk and cream, stirring constantly. Add the salt, pepper, cayenne, Worcestershire sauce and paprika, and stir well.

Return the pan to the heat and, stirring constantly, bring the sauce to the boil. Boil for 1 minute, stirring, or until the sauce is thick. Stir in the cheese. Remove from the heat and keep hot.

Preheat the grill [broiler] to high.

Line the grill [broiler] pan with aluminium foil. Place the toast slices on the foil. Set aside.

In a frying-pan, melt the butter over moderate heat. Add the ham to the pan and heat it for 2 minutes on each side.

Remove the slices of ham from the pan and place them on the slices of toast.

Top each slice of ham with a poached egg and spoon the hot sauce over the eggs. Place the grill [broiler] pan under the heat and grill [broil] for 1 to 2 minutes or until the sauce is golden and bubbling.

Remove the pan from the heat and serve immediately.

Egg Mousse

A delightful dish for a summer buffet lunch, this Egg Mousse is surprisingly easy to prepare.

8-10 SERVINGS

1 teaspoon vegetable oil
½ oz. gelatine
3 fl. oz. [⅜ cup] white wine
2 egg yolks, at room temperature
1 teaspoon salt
¾ teaspoon dry mustard
⅛ teaspoon white pepper
8 fl. oz. [1 cup] olive oil, at room temperature
1 tablespoon lemon juice or white wine vinegar
6 to 8 anchovies, soaked in milk for 10 minutes, drained and finely chopped
1 large onion, finely chopped
1 tablespoon chopped fresh parsley
1 tablespoon chopped fresh chives
10 hard-boiled eggs, chopped
8 fl. oz. [1 cup] béchamel sauce
8 fl. oz. double cream [1 cup heavy cream], lightly beaten
¼ teaspoon cayenne pepper
½ teaspoon paprika
10 stuffed olives, sliced

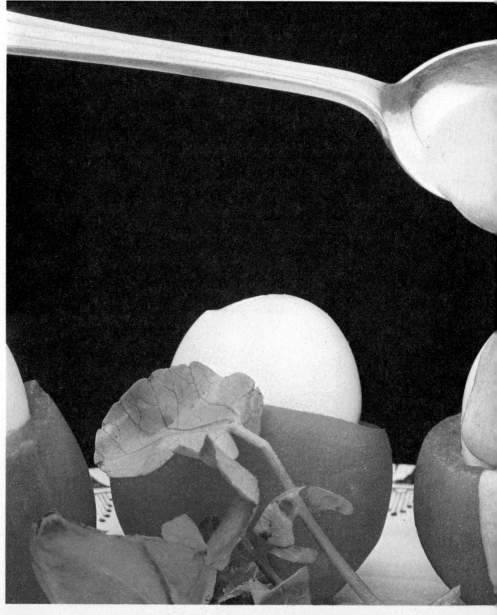

Using the oil, grease a 2½-pint [1½-quart] mould. Turn the mould upside down on kitchen paper towels to drain out any excess oil.

Place the gelatine in a heatproof mixing bowl. Add the wine and place the bowl over a pan of simmering water. Stir constantly to dissolve the gelatine. Remove from the heat.

Place the egg yolks, ½ teaspoon salt, the mustard and pepper in a mixing bowl. Using a wire whisk, beat the ingredients until they are thoroughly blended. Add the oil, a few drops at a time, whisking constantly. Do not add the oil too quickly or the mayonnaise will curdle. After the mayonnaise has thickened the oil may be added a little more rapidly.

Beat in a few drops of lemon juice or

Elegant Portuguese Eggs in Tomato Shells may be served cold, as a first course to a special dinner.

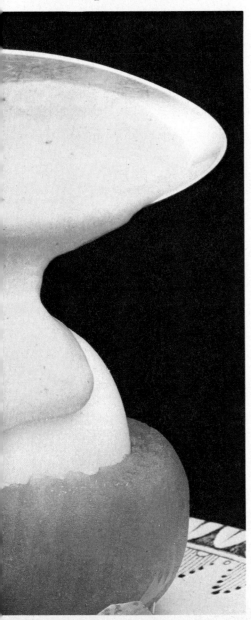

vinegar from time to time to prevent the mayonnaise from becoming too thick. When all the oil has been added, stir in the remaining lemon juice or vinegar. Taste for seasoning and add more salt, mustard and vinegar if desired.

Stir the anchovies, onion, parsley, chives, eggs and dissolved gelatine into the mayonnaise. Fold in the béchamel sauce with the cream, cayenne, paprika and the remaining salt.

Pour the mixture into the mould and place it in the refrigerator. Leave to chill for at least 2 hours or until it is completely set.

Run a knife round the edge of the mould and dip it quickly into hot water. Reverse the mould on to a serving dish, giving a sharp shake. The mousse should then slide out easily.

Garnish with the olives and serve.

Portuguese Eggs in Tomato Shells

☆   ①   ✕

Portuguese Eggs in Tomato Shells are eaten cold as a first course, or with a mixed green salad as a light lunch.

6 SERVINGS

6 large firm tomatoes, blanched and peeled
1 teaspoon salt
½ teaspoon black pepper
2 tablespoons olive oil
1 small onion, finely chopped
2 teaspoons chopped fresh basil
1 tablespoon tomato purée
6 hard-boiled eggs
4 tablespoons mayonnaise
watercress

Cut a circle out of the stalk end of each tomato so that there will be an opening big enough to insert an egg. With a teaspoon, scoop out the pulp and seeds. Reserve the pulp, seeds and lids. Sprinkle the insides of the scooped-out tomatoes with half the salt and pepper.

In a saucepan, heat the oil over moderate heat. When the oil is hot, add the onion and fry, stirring occasionally, for 5 to 7 minutes or until the onion is soft and translucent but not brown. Add the reserved tomato pulp and seeds, tomato lids, basil, tomato purée and the remaining salt and pepper. Reduce the heat to low, cover and simmer for 20 minutes or until the mixture is thick.

Remove the pan from the heat and set the sauce aside to cool.

Place the tomato shells on a serving dish. Place a hard-boiled egg in each shell. Place the dish in the refrigerator and chill for at least 20 minutes.

When the sauce is cold, stir in the mayonnaise. Transfer the sauce to a small mixing bowl and place it in the refrigerator to chill.

Remove the tomato shells and sauce from the refrigerator. Spoon the sauce over the eggs, garnish with watercress and serve.

Egg Ratatouille

☆   ① ①   ✕ ✕

An unusual dish to serve for a light supper, Egg Ratatouille needs no accompaniment other than crusty bread and butter.

4 SERVINGS

2 large aubergines [eggplants], washed and sliced
2½ teaspoons salt
1 lb. courgettes [zucchini], washed and sliced
2 fl. oz. [¼ cup] olive oil
1 large onion, sliced and pushed out into rings
1 large garlic clove, crushed
1 green pepper, white pith removed, seeded and sliced
4 tomatoes, blanched, peeled and chopped
4 oz. mushrooms, sliced
¼ teaspoon black pepper
¼ teaspoon dried basil
1 oz. [2 tablespoons] butter
4 eggs

Place the aubergine [eggplant] slices in a colander and sprinkle over 1 teaspoon of salt. Leave them to dégorge for 30 minutes. Place the courgette [zucchini] slices on a plate and sprinkle over 1 teaspoon salt. Set aside for 30 minutes to dégorge.

Dry the slices on kitchen paper towels.

In a very large saucepan, heat the olive oil over moderate heat. When the oil is hot, add the onion and garlic and fry for 5 to 7 minutes or until the onion is soft and translucent but not brown. Add the courgettes [zucchini], aubergines [eggplants] and pepper to the pan and cook for 10 minutes. Stir in the tomatoes and mushrooms and sprinkle over the remaining salt, the pepper and basil. Half cover the pan with the lid on a slant, reduce the heat to low and simmer the ratatouille, stirring occasionally, for 45 minutes.

Five minutes before the ratatouille is ready, in a large frying-pan, melt the butter over moderate heat. Break the eggs into the pan and fry them for 4 to 5 minutes or until the whites are set.

Turn the ratatouille into a warmed serving dish. Top the mixture with the fried eggs and serve at once.

Quick-Fried Eggs with Petits Pois and Shrimps

☆ ① ① ✕

An adaptation of a traditional Chinese dish, Quick-Fried Eggs with Petits Pois and Shrimps may be served as part of a Chinese meal, or accompanied by ice-cold lager and green salad, as a light lunch or supper.

2-3 SERVINGS

5 eggs
1 teaspoon salt
1 oz. [2 tablespoons] butter
1-inch piece fresh root ginger, peeled and chopped
1 medium-sized onion, thinly sliced
4 oz. small frozen shrimps, thawed
8 oz. frozen petits pois, thawed
1 tablespoon soy sauce
½ teaspoon sugar
2 tablespoons vegetable oil

In a medium-sized mixing bowl, beat the eggs and salt together until they are well blended. Set aside.

In a medium-sized saucepan, melt the butter over moderate heat. When the foam subsides, add the ginger and onion and stir-fry for 30 seconds. Add the shrimps, petits pois, soy sauce and sugar and stir-fry the mixture for 1½ minutes. Remove the pan from the heat and set the mixture

aside.

In a large frying-pan, heat the oil over moderate heat. When the oil is hot, pour the egg mixture into the pan. Stir the eggs, then leave for a few seconds until the bottom sets. Remove the pan from the heat and pour in the shrimps and petits pois. Turn, mix and toss the mixture a few times. Return the pan to the heat and cook, stirring occasionally, for 1 minute. Remove the pan from the heat.

Transfer the mixture to a warmed serving dish and serve at once.

Ricotta and Olive Mix

☆ ① ① ✕

A quick and relatively inexpensive way of brightening up scrambled eggs, Ricotta and Olive Mix may be served for breakfast or, with crusty bread, for a light lunch.

2-3 SERVINGS

3 tablespoons olive oil
4 oz. [1 cup] green olives, stoned and quartered
1 red pepper, white pith removed, seeded and chopped
4 oz. ricotta cheese, crumbled
6 eggs
4 tablespoons milk
½ teaspoon freshly ground black pepper

Ricotta and Olive Mix is a nutritious mixture of eggs, green olives, red pepper and ricotta cheese. Serve with lots of hot toast.

½ teaspoon dried basil
2 oz. [½ cup] Parmesan cheese, grated

Preheat the grill [broiler] to moderately high.

In a shallow, flameproof casserole, heat the olive oil over moderate heat. When the oil is hot, add the olives and red pepper and cook, stirring frequently, for 3 minutes. Add the ricotta cheese and, stirring constantly, cook for a further 2 minutes.

Meanwhile, in a medium-sized mixing bowl, lightly beat the eggs, milk, pepper and basil together.

Reduce the heat to low. Add the egg mixture and cook, stirring constantly, until the eggs are nearly scrambled.

Remove the casserole from the heat. Sprinkle over the Parmesan cheese and place the casserole under the grill [broiler] and grill [broil] for 3 minutes or until the cheese has melted and the top is lightly browned.

Remove the casserole from the grill [broiler] and serve at once.

Russian Coloured Eggs

☆　　①　　⧗

Exchanging eggs at Easter is a world-wide custom dating back to pre-Christian times. It became very fashionable in Imperialist Russia when Tzar Alexander III presented his wife with an expensive jewelled egg, designed and made by the court jeweller, Karl Fabergé. On a more humble level, ordinary Russians, particularly Ukrainians, adopted the fashion and, over the years, attained a high standard of artistic skill in decorating and dyeing ordinary egg shells.

To make Russian Coloured Eggs natural vegetable dye or food colouring should be used. Place only white-shelled eggs in a saucepan containing the chosen dye (see the colour guide which follows for further information on this) and bring the liquid to the boil. Simmer the eggs

These traditional Russian Coloured Eggs are so pretty to look at, yet so easy to decorate.

over low heat for 10 minutes. Remove the pan from the heat and, using a slotted spoon, remove the eggs from the pan. Pat the eggs dry with kitchen paper towels and set aside to cool.

If they are to remain a plain colour, rub the eggs with vegetable oil. If they are to be further hand painted, rub them with vegetable oil when decoration is complete.

COLOUR GUIDE FOR NATURAL VEGETABLE DYES

The outer skins of
onions boiled in water......deep yellow
Raw beetroots [beets]
boiled in water.............red, pink
Birch leaves boiled
in water..................... green
Moss-down boiled in water..light green

Alternatively, a few drops of edible food colouring can be added to the water.

DECORATING THE EGGS

Onion skins wrapped around the eggs and tied on with cotton thread develop

a marbled effect when the skins are removed.

Eggs wrapped in silk material and tied with cotton take on a 'tie-dye' effect when the material is removed.

Thin strips of masking tape stuck on to the eggs in varying geometric and flower patterns, before boiling, will reveal patterns in white when the tape is removed.

Flower petals stuck to damp, uncooked eggs and then covered with onion or shallot skins, tied with cotton thread, produce yellow flower-patterned eggs.

Dental floss or cotton thread rubbed in beeswax and wound around the eggs, then removed when the egg is cold, produces a myriad of lined patterns. Alternatively, unwaxed cotton thread wound around the eggs produces a myriad of deeper coloured patterned lines.

Eggs which are simply simmered gently in an edible food colour may be hand-painted with other edible food colours to any design imaginable.

The eggs should be eaten within 48 hours of decoration.

Egg Salad

☆ ① ⊠

This unusual and attractive salad may be served either as an addition to a light fish dish or by itself with hot crusty bread as an interesting summer lunch.

2-4 SERVINGS

6 hard-boiled eggs, sliced
2 small green peppers, white pith removed, seeded and roughly chopped
1 pimiento, cut into strips
3 button mushrooms, wiped clean and thinly sliced
6 black olives, stoned
1 tablespoon finely chopped walnuts

DRESSING

1 small garlic clove, crushed
1 teaspoon paprika
2 tablespoons white wine vinegar
6 tablespoons olive oil
¼ teaspoon salt
⅛ teaspoon black pepper
½ teaspoon sugar

Arrange the eggs, peppers, pimiento, mushrooms and olives in a medium-sized serving dish. Sprinkle the walnuts over the ingredients.

This colourful Egg Salad, with its spicy garlic-flavoured dressing, makes an inexpensive, satisfying lunch or supper.

In a screw-top jar, combine all the ingredients for the dressing. Shake briskly and pour the dressing over the salad. Toss to coat the ingredients well with the dressing.

Chill for at least 30 minutes before serving.

Egg, Sausage and Pepper Casserole

☆ ① ⊠

This piquant and filling casserole, flavoured with spices and herbs, makes an interesting supper dish.

4 SERVINGS

1 teaspoon butter
3 tablespoons vegetable oil
2 medium-sized onions, thinly sliced
1 medium-sized red pepper, white pith removed, seeded and finely sliced
1 medium-sized green pepper, white pith removed, seeded and finely sliced
2 large tomatoes, blanched, peeled and sliced
1 teaspoon paprika
½ teaspoon dried thyme
½ teaspoon salt
¼ teaspoon black pepper
8 beef or pork sausages
8 eggs
½ teaspoon prepared English mustard

1 tablespoon tomato purée
4 fl. oz. [½ cup] tomato juice
3 tablespoons grated Parmesan cheese

Preheat the oven to moderate 350°F (Gas Mark 4, 180°C).

Grease a large baking dish with the butter.

In a medium-sized frying-pan heat 2 tablespoons of the oil over moderate heat. When the oil is hot, add the onions, red and green peppers, tomatoes, paprika, thyme, salt and black pepper. Fry, stirring occasionally, for 8 to 10 minutes or until the onions and peppers are soft and golden and the tomatoes are pulpy. Turn the mixture into the greased baking dish and set aside.

Heat the remaining oil in the frying-pan. When the oil is hot, place the sausages in the pan and fry them for 5 minutes or until they are browned all over. Remove the pan from the heat and arrange the sausages on top of the vegetables, leaving a gap between each one. Carefully break one egg into each of the gaps.

In a small mixing bowl, combine the mustard and tomato purée. Stir in the tomato juice and pour the mixture over the ingredients in the baking dish. Sprinkle the cheese on top.

Bake in the centre of the oven for 20 to 30 minutes, or until the eggs are set and the sausages cooked. Remove from the oven and serve hot.

Shirred Eggs

Shirred Eggs are eggs which are broken into a buttered flameproof dish and baked, fried or grilled [broiled] quickly.

Shirred Eggs make an excellent light, nourishing snack, first course, or breakfast dish.

4 SERVINGS

1½ oz. [3 tablespoons] butter
8 large eggs
½ teaspoon salt
¼ teaspoon freshly ground black
   pepper

Preheat the grill [broiler] to high.

In a large flameproof dish or shallow flameproof casserole, melt the butter over moderately low heat. When the foam subsides, break in the eggs, being careful not to break the yolks. Tilt the dish or casserole so that the butter runs over the eggs. Cook for 1 minute.

Remove the dish or casserole from the heat and place it under the grill [broiler]. Grill [broil] for 3 minutes, basting occasionally with the butter, or until the whites have set and a thin film covers the yolks.

Remove the dish or casserole from the heat. Season with the salt and pepper and serve at once.

Egg Tartlets ✓

These delicious little tartlets are made with shortcrust pastry and are filled with chopped eggs and topped with a garlic, basil and mayonnaise sauce. They make an ideal hors d'oeuvre or first course, and are especially suitable for a dinner party as the pastry cases and mayonnaise can be made well in advance then filled just before serving.

6 SERVINGS

PASTRY
6 oz. [1½ cups] flour
⅛ teaspoon salt
1½ oz. [3 tablespoons] plus 2
   teaspoons butter
1½ oz. [3 tablespoons] vegetable fat
1 to 2 tablespoons iced water
FILLING
10 fl. oz. [1¼ cups] mayonnaise
1 large garlic clove, crushed
4 tablespoons coarsely chopped
   fresh basil
4 hard-boiled eggs, finely chopped
GARNISH
6 slices hard-boiled egg
6 small basil sprigs

Preheat the oven to fairly hot 400°F

(Gas Mark 6, 200°C).

First make the pastry. Sift the flour and salt into a medium-sized mixing bowl. Add 1½ ounces [3 tablespoons] of the butter and the vegetable fat and cut them into small pieces with a table knife. With your fingertips, rub the fat into the flour until the mixture resembles fine breadcrumbs.

Add 1 tablespoon of iced water and, using the knife, mix it into the flour mixture. With your hands, mix and knead the dough until it is smooth. Add more water if the dough is too dry. Chill the dough in the refrigerator for 30 minutes.

Using the remaining butter, grease 6 3-inch fluted tartlet tins. Set aside.

To make the filling, blend the mayonnaise, garlic and chopped basil together. Set aside.

On a lightly floured surface roll out the dough to ¼ inch thick. Using a 4-inch round pastry cutter, cut the dough into 6 circles. Line the tartlet tins with the dough circles, easing the dough in carefully. With a knife, trim off the excess dough. Fill the pastry cases with crumpled greaseproof or waxed paper and place them in the oven. Bake blind for 15 minutes, removing the paper 5 minutes before the baking time is completed to allow the pastry to brown.

Remove the tins from the oven and leave to cool for 30 minutes. Turn the pastry cases out of the tins.

Half-fill the pastry cases with chopped hard-boiled eggs. Pour enough of the mayonnaise mixture over the eggs just to fill the pastry cases.

Decorate each tartlet with 1 slice of hard-boiled egg and a sprig of basil. Serve cold.

These pretty little Egg Tartlets contain a creamy mixture of eggs with garlic and basil in a mayonnaise sauce. Serve them as a filling first course to a formal dinner.

Weston Eggs

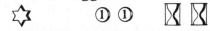

A delicious, mousse-like first course, Weston Eggs are very simple to make. Serve with croûtons or melba toast.

4-6 SERVINGS

8 oz. spaghetti, cooked for 8 to 10
   minutes and thoroughly
   drained
4 hard-boiled eggs
2 tablespoons mayonnaise
1 tablespoon tomato purée
½ teaspoon salt
½ teaspoon freshly ground black
   pepper
8 fl. oz. double cream [1 cup
   heavy cream]
1 hard-boiled egg yolk

Push the spaghetti and the eggs through a food mill or, alternatively, purée them in a blender.

Place the mixture in a medium-sized mixing bowl and, using a wooden spoon, gradually stir in the mayonnaise, tomato purée, salt, black pepper and cream, beating until all the ingredients are thoroughly combined.

Transfer the mixture to a small soufflé dish and place the dish in the refrigerator to chill for 1 hour.

Remove the dish from the refrigerator and crumble the remaining egg yolk over the top.

Serve at once.

Frittata di Carne e Vegetali

VEGETABLE AND MEAT OMELET

An economical and easy supper dish, Frittata de Carne e Vegetali may be served at an informal dinner. It is a firm omelet and should be cut like a cake. The vegetables used here are typically Italian, but any other chopped vegetables may be used.

4 SERVINGS

1 oz. [2 tablespoons] butter
1 tablespoon olive oil
1 onion, finely chopped
2 courgettes [zucchini], trimmed, washed and sliced
2 large tomatoes, blanched, peeled, seeded and finely chopped
6 oz. cooked ham, finely chopped
6 eggs
¼ teaspoon salt
¼ teaspoon dried oregano
¼ teaspoon dried marjoram
½ teaspoon black pepper
2 oz. [½ cup] Provolone cheese, grated

In a large omelet pan, melt the butter with the oil over moderate heat. When the foam subsides, add the onion and fry it for 8 to 10 minutes, or until it is golden. Add the courgettes [zucchini] to the pan and fry for 4 minutes, turning occasional-

ly. Add the tomatoes and ham and cook the mixture for a further 4 minutes.

Meanwhile, break the eggs into a small bowl. Add the salt, oregano, marjoram and pepper and beat to blend.

Preheat the grill [broiler] to high.

Increase the heat under the omelet pan to moderately high. Pour the beaten eggs over the vegetables in the pan. Allow the base to set, reduce the heat to low and continue cooking the omelet until the eggs are just about to set on top. Sprinkle over the cheese and remove the pan from the heat. Place it under the grill [broiler] and cook for 2 minutes, or until the cheese has melted. Cut the omelet into quarters and serve.

Javanese Omelet

Unlike the traditional light fluffy French omelets, Javanese Omelet is a spicy version, cooked until it is completely set and golden brown. It may be served on its own as a light supper snack.

2-4 SERVINGS

6 eggs
1 tablespoon cold water
½ teaspoon salt
1 tablespoon soy sauce
1 teaspoon soft brown sugar

Frittata di Carne e Vegetali.

2 tablespoons vegetable oil
1 small onion, finely chopped
2 green chillis, seeds removed and finely sliced

In a mixing bowl, beat the eggs, water, salt, soy sauce and sugar together with a wire whisk or rotary beater until the mixture is light and foamy.

In an omelet pan, heat the oil over moderate heat. Add the onion and chillis. Cook, stirring occasionally, until they are soft but not brown.

Onion and Aubergine [Eggplant] Omelet

An unusual supper dish, Onion and Aubergine [Eggplant] Omelet is adapted from an Iranian recipe. Serve with a tomato salad.

2-3 SERVINGS

3 tablespoons vegetable oil
1 onion, finely chopped
1 medium-sized aubergine [eggplant], cut into ¾-inch cubes and dégorged
½ teaspoon turmeric
¼ teaspoon ground cumin
¾ teaspoon salt
½ teaspoon black pepper
4 eggs
1½ tablespoons cold water
1 tablespoon butter

In a medium-sized frying-pan, heat the oil over moderate heat. When the oil is hot, add the onion and fry, stirring occasionally, for 8 to 10 minutes or until it is golden brown.

Add the aubergine [eggplant] cubes and cook them, stirring constantly, for 3 minutes. Stir in the turmeric, cumin, ½ teaspoon of the salt and ¼ teaspoon of the pepper. Reduce the heat to low and simmer the aubergine [eggplant] mixture for 10 minutes or until the aubergine [eggplant] cubes are tender. Set aside.

In a medium-sized mixing bowl, beat the eggs, the remaining salt and pepper and the water together with a fork. Add the aubergine [eggplant] mixture and beat until the ingredients are well mixed.

In a medium-sized omelet pan, melt the butter over moderate heat. When the foam subsides, pour in the egg mixture. Stir the eggs, then leave them for a few seconds until the bottom sets. Reduce the heat to low. Using a palette knife or spatula, lift the edge of the omelet and, at the same time, tilt the pan away from you so that the liquid egg escapes from the top and runs into the pan. Put the pan down flat over the heat and leave until the omelet begins to set.

Invert a medium-sized plate over the omelet pan and reverse the two. The omelet should fall on to the plate. Slide the omelet back into the pan, so that the browned side is uppermost, and continue cooking for 1 minute or until the omelet is completely set.

Slide the omelet on to a heated serving dish. Cut into wedges and serve immediately.

Tilt the pan and pour in the beaten egg mixture. Cook until the eggs are almost set. With a flat-bladed knife, lift the edges of the setting omelet and tilt the pan so that the remaining liquid seeps to the bottom.

When the omelet is completely set, continue cooking it for 3 to 5 minutes, or until it is golden brown on the bottom.

Remove the pan from the heat and slide the omelet on to a warmed serving plate. Serve at once.

Pipérade
PEPPER AND TOMATO OMELET

☆   ①   ⋈

One of the great classic French regional dishes, Pipérade originated in the Basque country near Béarn. Serve Pipérade with some crusty French bread, a tossed lettuce salad and some vin ordinaire.

2 SERVINGS

2 fl. oz. [¼ cup] olive oil
1 small onion, finely chopped
2 garlic cloves, crushed
1 green pepper, white pith removed, seeded and chopped
1 red pepper, white pith removed, seeded and chopped
3 tomatoes, blanched, peeled, seeded and chopped
6 eggs
¼ teaspoon salt
¼ teaspoon black pepper
2 tablespoons water

In a large omelet pan or frying-pan, heat the oil over moderate heat. When the oil is hot, add the onion, garlic and peppers and cook, stirring occasionally, for 5 to 7 minutes or until the onion is soft and translucent but not brown. Stir in the tomatoes and cook, stirring occasionally, for 5 minutes.

Meanwhile, in a large mixing bowl, beat the eggs, salt, pepper and water together until they are well mixed.

Pour the egg mixture into the pan. Stir the eggs, then leave them for a few seconds until the bottom sets. Reduce the heat to low. Using a palette knife or spatula, lift the edges of the omelet and, at the same time, tilt the pan away from you so that the liquid egg escapes from the top and runs on to the pan. Put the pan down flat over the heat and leave until the omelet begins to set again.

Remove the pan from the heat and, with the help of the palette knife, slide the pipérade quickly on to a warmed serving dish. Cut into two and serve at once.

Classic French Pipérade.

✓ Courgette [Zucchini] Soufflé

☆ ☆ ① ⋈ ⋈

Like most soufflés, Courgette [Zucchini] Soufflé is an extremely light and fluffy main course dish. Serve with a vegetable salad and some well-chilled white wine, such as Muscadet or Chablis.

4 SERVINGS

1½ oz. [3 tablespoons] butter
4 tablespoons olive oil
8 medium-sized courgettes [zucchini], trimmed, blanched and sliced
½ teaspoon salt
1 teaspoon freshly ground black pepper
1 garlic clove, crushed
2 oz. [⅔ cup] fine dry breadcrumbs
4 egg yolks
3 oz. [¾ cup] plus 1 tablespoon Parmesan cheese, grated
1 tablespoon prepared French mustard
2 tablespoons flour
4 fl. oz. single cream [½ cup light cream]
6 egg whites, stiffly beaten
1 tablespoon finely chopped fresh parsley

Using 1 tablespoon of the butter, grease a 2½-pint [1½-quart] soufflé dish and set aside.

In a large frying-pan, heat the olive oil over moderate heat. When the oil is hot, add the courgettes [zucchini] to the pan and fry them, stirring occasionally, for 10 minutes.

Raise the heat to moderately high and stir in the salt, half the black pepper, the garlic and dry breadcrumbs. Remove the pan from the heat and toss the courgette [zucchini] slices gently. Transfer the mixture to a fine wire strainer held over a medium-sized mixing bowl. Using the back of a wooden spoon, rub the ingredients through the strainer. Discard any pulp remaining in the strainer. Alternatively, place the courgette [zucchini] mixture in the jar of an electric blender and blend on and off until the mixture forms a fine purée.

Place the purée in the refrigerator to chill for 1 hour.

Preheat the oven to very hot 450°F (Gas Mark 8, 230°C).

Meanwhile, in a medium-sized mixing bowl, beat the egg yolks, 3 ounces [¾ cup] of the cheese, the remaining pepper and the mustard together with a wooden spoon until the ingredients are thoroughly combined. Set aside.

In a medium-sized saucepan, melt the remaining butter over moderate heat. Remove the pan from the heat and, using

a wooden spoon, stir in the flour to form a smooth paste. Gradually add the cream, stirring constantly and being careful to avoid lumps. Return the pan to moderately low heat and cook, stirring constantly, for 2 to 3 minutes or until the mixture thickens. Remove the pan from the heat and set aside to cool.

When the mixture is cool, stir in the egg yolk mixture. Remove the purée from the refrigerator and stir 8 fluid ounces [1 cup] of the purée into the sauce. Discard any remaining purée or set aside for future use. With a metal spoon, gently fold in the beaten egg whites. Transfer the mixture to the prepared soufflé dish and sprinkle the top with the remaining cheese. Place the dish in the centre of the oven and cook for 10 minutes.

Reduce the heat to fairly hot 400°F (Gas Mark 6, 200°C) and continue to

The unusual combination of pears and carrots give this Pear and Carrot Soufflé its unusual flavour. Serve with salad for a delicious meal.

cook for 20 minutes or until the soufflé has risen and is golden brown, and a skewer inserted into the centre comes out clean.

Remove the soufflé dish from the oven. Sprinkle over the chopped parsley and serve immediately.

Pear and Carrot Soufflé

☆ ☆ ① ⋈ ⋈

Pear and Carrot Soufflé is a superb light and fluffy main course dish, with special appeal for vegetarians. Serve with lots of

tossed mixed salad and crusty bread and a chilled sparkling wine such as Blanc de Blancs or vinho verde.

4 SERVINGS

5 medium-sized carrots, scraped and grated
4 soft pears, peeled, cored and chopped
2 fl. oz. [¼ cup] water
1½ oz. [3 tablespoons] butter
4 egg yolks
4 oz. [1 cup] plus 1 teaspoon Parmesan cheese, grated
½ teaspoon freshly ground black pepper
1 tablespoon prepared French mustard
2 tablespoons flour
4 fl. oz. single cream [½ cup light cream]
6 egg whites, stiffly beaten

Place the carrots, pears and water in a medium-sized saucepan. Set the pan over moderate heat and bring the liquid to the boil. Cover the pan, reduce the heat to low and simmer for 20 minutes. Remove the pan from the heat and set the mixture aside to cool.

Place the mixture in a fine wire strainer held over a medium-sized mixing bowl. Using the back of a wooden spoon, rub the ingredients through the strainer, discarding any pulp remaining in the strainer. Alternatively, place the carrot and pear mixture in the jar of an electric blender and blend on and off until the mixture forms a fine purée.

Place the purée in the refrigerator to chill for 1 hour.

Preheat the oven to very hot 450°F (Gas Mark 8, 230°C). Using 1 tablespoon of the butter, grease a 4-pint [2½-quart] soufflé dish and set aside.

Meanwhile, in a medium-sized mixing bowl, beat the egg yolks, 4 ounces [1 cup] of the cheese, the pepper and mustard together with a wooden spoon until all the ingredients are thoroughly combined. Set aside.

In a medium-sized saucepan, melt the remaining butter over moderate heat. Remove the pan from the heat and, using a wooden spoon, stir in the flour to make a smooth paste. Gradually add the cream, stirring constantly and being careful to avoid lumps. Return the pan to moderately low heat and cook, stirring constantly, for 2 to 3 minutes or until the mixture thickens. Remove the pan from the heat and set the mixture aside to cool.

When the mixture is cool, stir in the egg yolk mixture. Remove the purée from the refrigerator and add 8 fluid ounces [1 cup] of the purée to the sauce. Blend the mixture together. With a metal spoon, gently fold in the beaten egg whites. Transfer the mixture to the prepared soufflé dish and sprinkle the top with the remaining cheese.

Place the dish in the centre of the oven and cook for 10 minutes.

Reduce the heat to fairly hot 400°F (Gas Mark 6, 200°C) and continue to cook for 20 minutes or until the soufflé has risen and is golden brown, and a skewer inserted into the centre comes out clean. Remove the soufflé dish from the oven.

Pour the remaining purée into a sauce-boat and serve immediately, with the soufflé.

Salmon Soufflé

☆ ☆   ① ①   ⊠

A delightful way to use up leftover cooked fresh salmon, if you happen to be lucky enough to have it (canned salmon is nearly as delicious if you aren't), Salmon Soufflé may be served as a light supper dish accompanied by a mixed salad, brown bread and butter and some well-chilled white wine, such as Chablis.

4 SERVINGS

1½ oz. [3 tablespoons] butter
10 oz. cooked fresh salmon, skinned, boned and flaked
    or 12 oz. canned salmon, drained
3 fl. oz. single cream [⅜ cup light cream]
1 oz. [¼ cup] flour
10 fl. oz. [1¼ cups] milk
2 oz. [½ cup] Gruyère cheese, finely grated
½ teaspoon salt
½ teaspoon freshly ground black pepper
¼ teaspoon Tabasco sauce
4 egg yolks
5 egg whites

Preheat the oven to fairly hot 375°F (Gas Mark 5, 190°C). Using 1 tablespoon of butter, grease a 2½-pint [1½-quart] soufflé dish. Set aside.

Using the back of a wooden spoon, rub the salmon through a fine wire strainer into a medium-sized mixing bowl. Gradually beat the cream into the salmon purée. Set aside.

Alternatively, put the salmon and cream in an electric blender and blend on and off at high speed until the mixture forms a purée. Set aside.

In a medium-sized saucepan, melt the remaining butter over moderate heat. Remove the pan from the heat and, using a wooden spoon, stir in the flour to make a smooth paste. Gradually add the milk, stirring constantly. Return the pan to moderately low heat and cook the sauce, stirring constantly with the spoon, until it is thick and smooth. Remove the pan from the heat and add the salmon purée, the cheese, salt, black pepper and Tabasco sauce. Set the mixture aside to cool to lukewarm, then beat in the egg yolks, one by one.

In a large mixing bowl, beat the egg whites with a wire whisk or rotary beater until they form stiff peaks. With a metal spoon, carefully fold the beaten egg whites into the mixture.

Spoon the mixture into the prepared soufflé dish.

Place the dish in the centre of the oven and bake for 25 to 30 minutes or until the soufflé has risen and is golden brown, and a skewer inserted into the centre comes out clean.

Remove the soufflé from the oven and serve immediately.

Icicles

☆ ① ⧖ ⧖

Attractive meringue biscuits [cookies], Icicles make a delicious coffee-break snack.

15 BISCUITS [COOKIES]

2 oz. [¼ cup] plus 1 teaspoon butter
2 oz. [¼ cup] sugar
3 oz. [¾ cup] flour
1 oz. cornflour [¼ cup cornstarch]
3 teaspoons water
½ teaspoon vanilla essence
2 oz. apricot jam
1 teaspoon lemon juice
MERINGUE
2 egg whites
4 oz. [½ cup] castor sugar

Preheat the oven to moderate 350°F (Gas Mark 4, 180°C).

Using the teaspoon of butter, grease two large baking sheets.

In a medium-sized mixing bowl, cream the remaining butter with a wooden spoon until it is soft. Add the sugar and beat until the mixture is light and fluffy. Sift the flour and cornflour [cornstarch] on to the mixture, and mix it in with a metal spoon. Mix in the water and the vanilla essence. Lightly knead the dough.

On a lightly floured surface, roll out the dough to a circle about ¼-inch thick. Using a 1½-inch pastry cutter, cut out circles of the dough and place them on the baking sheets. Place the baking sheets in the oven and bake for 8 minutes or until the biscuits [cookies] are a light golden brown.

While the biscuits [cookies] are baking, prepare the meringue. In a large mixing bowl, beat the egg whites with a wire whisk or rotary beater until they form stiff peaks. Add 1 tablespoon of the sugar and continue beating for 1 minute. Using a metal spoon, carefully fold in the remaining sugar.

Remove the biscuits [cookies] from the oven and set them aside to cool slightly.

In a small mixing bowl, mix together the apricot jam and lemon juice. Place a small teaspoonful of the jam mixture in the centre of each biscuit [cookie].

Place a ½-inch star nozzle in a large forcing bag and fill the bag with the meringue mixture. Pipe swirls of meringue on to the biscuits [cookies], covering them completely and pulling the last squeeze up into a point.

Return the baking sheets to the oven and bake for 8 minutes or until the meringue is set and lightly browned.

Remove the baking sheets from the oven and allow the icicles to cool slightly. Transfer the icicles to a wire rack and allow them to cool completely before serving.

Pavlova

☆ ☆ ① ① ⧖ ⧖

Pavlova is a famous meringue-based dessert, named after the Russian ballerina, Anna Pavlova. It was created in honour of her performance of the Dying Swan in Swan Lake which she danced while touring Australia, and the dessert is now considered to be traditionally Australian.

ONE 9-INCH CAKE

5 egg whites
10 oz. [1¼ cups] plus 1 tablespoon castor sugar
2 teaspoons cornflour [cornstarch], sifted
½ teaspoon vanilla essence
1 teaspoon malt vinegar
1 teaspoon orange-flavoured liqueur
10 fl. oz. double cream [1¼ cups heavy cream], stiffly whipped
1 lb. fresh or canned and drained fruit

Preheat the oven to cool 300°F (Gas Mark 2, 150°C). With a pencil draw a 9-inch circle on a piece of non-stick silicone paper and place this on a baking sheet.

In a large mixing bowl, beat the egg whites with a wire whisk or rotary beater until they form stiff peaks. Beat in 4 ounces [½ cup] of the sugar and continue beating until the mixture is very stiff and glossy. Fold in all but 1 tablespoon of the remaining sugar, the cornflour [cornstarch], vanilla essence and vinegar.

Spoon one-third of the mixture on to the circle of paper to make a base about ¼-inch thick. Fill a forcing bag, fitted with a 1-inch nozzle, with the remaining mixture and pipe it round the edge of the circle in decorative swirls, to form a case.

Place the baking sheet in the oven and bake for 1 hour. Turn off the oven and leave the meringue in the oven for a further 30 minutes, or until it is crisp on the outside but still soft in the centre.

Remove the baking sheet from the oven. Leave the meringue to cool completely. When it is cold, lift it off the baking sheet and carefully remove and discard the paper from the bottom.

Place the meringue case on a serving plate. Fold the orange-flavoured liqueur and the remaining tablespoon of sugar into the cream. Spoon the cream into the centre of the meringue case and pile the fruit on top of the cream. Serve at once.

Pineapple and Meringue Soufflé

☆ ① ① ⧖ ⧖

This delicately flavoured dish makes a

To make Pavlova, draw a 9-inch circle on non-stick silicone paper (use a plate or board as guide).

When the meringue mixture is stiff, spread one-third over the circle to make a base about ¼-inch thick.

Using a forcing bag with a 1-inch nozzle, pipe the remaining mixture around the edge of the circle.

When the meringue case has cooked and cooled completely, transfer it to a serving plate.

decorative dessert for a formal dinner.

4 SERVINGS

1 pint [2½ cups] milk
4 egg yolks
4 oz. [½ cup] castor sugar
¼ teaspoon vanilla essence
2 teaspoons grated lemon rind
2 tablespoons kirsch
5 oz. canned pineapple rings,
    drained and chopped
3 egg whites
1 tablespoon sifted icing
    [confectioners'] sugar

Preheat the oven to warm 325°F (Gas Mark 3, 170°C).

In a medium-sized saucepan, scald the milk over moderate heat. Set aside.

In a medium-sized mixing bowl, beat the egg yolks with a wire whisk or rotary beater until they are pale and thick. Beat in the sugar, vanilla essence, lemon rind and kirsch. Continue beating until the mixture is smooth. Very gradually, beating constantly, pour in the milk.

Place the pineapple in a 2-pint [1½-quart] baking dish. Pour the custard through a strainer over the pineapple. Cover the dish with foil. Put the dish in a roasting tin and pour in enough boiling

Stunning Pavlova - a meringue case filled with fruit.

water to come halfway up the sides of the dish. Place the tin in the centre of the oven. Bake the custard for 60 to 70 minutes or until it is just set.

Ten minutes before the custard is ready, prepare the meringue. In a medium-sized mixing bowl, beat the egg whites with a wire whisk or rotary beater until they form soft peaks. Add the icing [confectioners'] sugar and continue beating until the mixture forms stiff peaks.

Remove the tin from the oven. Spread the egg white mixture on top of the custard.

Replace the dish in the oven and bake for 15 to 20 minutes, or until the meringue is brown. Serve immediately.

Zabaglione Orientale

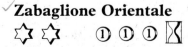

Zabaglione Orientale is a piquant variation of the traditional zabaglione. The distinctive orange flavour helps to counteract the richness of the eggs and sugar.

6 SERVINGS

6 ratafia biscuits [cookies]
4 fl. oz. [½ cup] orange-flavoured
    liqueur
2 tablespoons gin
1 tablespoon grated orange rind
4 egg yolks
4 tablespoons castor sugar

Place one ratafia biscuit [cookie] on the bottom of each of 6 serving glasses and distribute 2 fluid ounces [¼ cup] of orange liqueur evenly over them.

Pour the remaining orange liqueur and the gin into a cup. Add the orange rind and beat well with a fork.

In a heatproof mixing bowl, beat the egg yolks and sugar with a wire whisk or rotary beater until they thicken and become pale yellow. Put the bowl over a saucepan one-third full of boiling water and place the pan over moderate heat. Pour in the orange rind and gin mixture and continue beating until the mixture stiffens and rises slightly.

Remove the pan from the heat and remove the bowl from the pan. Pour equal quantities of the mixture into the serving glasses and serve the zabaglione immediately.

Cheese

WHAT CHEESE IS

The making of cheese was originally a method of preserving milk, but became popular for its own sake early in history. Cheese has kept its popularity ever since, being a relatively inexpensive, and very versatile and nourishing food. Cheese is a very valuable protein food, containing as it does high proportions of both protein and fat.

Cheese is made by curdling milk by adding a preparation of rennet or a particular starter culture which changes the milk into lactic acid during the cheese-making process. The curds are separated from the liquid whey and are then ripened in various ways. The milk used in Europe and America is usually that of cows, goats or ewes.

The processes used in the cheese-making and the climate and vegetation that produced the milk vary so greatly that many cheeses cannot be reproduced successfully outside their original districts. Others are more easily reproduced and are made commercially in large quantities.

THE COUNTRIES THAT PRODUCE CHEESE

The United States is the world's largest producer of cheese, making twice as much as France, its nearest rival. There are, however, only two well-known American

A wonderful and delicious variety of cheeses from England, Scotland, Wales, France, Holland, Switzerland, Denmark and Italy - choose a colourful selection of them to serve after your next dinner party.
1 Edam 2 Gouda 3 Danish Blue 4 Havarti 5 Samsoe 6 Esrom 7 Gruyère 8 Emmenthal 9 Caerphilly 10 Lancashire 11 Cheshire 12 Sage Derby 13 Caboc 14 Stilton 15 Dunlop 16 Cheddar 17 Derby 18 Roquefort 19 Port Salut 20 Camembert 21 Brie 22 Marc de Raisin 23 Parmesan 24 Mozzarella 25 Gorgonzola 26 Bel Paese.

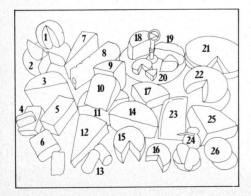

cheeses, the rest being either processed cheeses, or imitations of foreign varieties, although some of these are considered to be as good as, or even better than, their originals.

Liederkranz and Brick are the only well-known originally American cheeses. Liederkranz, aromatic and acid, was invented accidentally by Emil Frey, a New York cheese-maker. He was trying to duplicate a German cheese, but produced Liederkranz instead. He named his invention after a local singing society (the word means 'wreath of song').

Brick is little known outside the Middle West — it originated in Wisconsin, the leading American dairy state. When new it is mild in flavour, but it strengthens as it ages. A mature Brick is excellent with a glass of beer.

Great Britain produces several fine cheeses, of which the best-known are Cheddar, Cheshire and Stilton — one of the world's finest blue-veined cheeses. Cheddar — perhaps the most famous and versatile cheese in the world — is now produced commercially in large quantities all the year round and all over the world. Cheshire, the oldest English cheese, has a nutty, slightly salty flavour, and is rarely imitated successfully. Stilton, traditionally eaten with port and walnuts after a meal, is mellow and rich and has a dark, wrinkled skin.

There are several other well-known British cheeses. Caerphilly is one of these — a very soft, easily digested cheese, now made in the West of England, although it was originally Welsh. Derby, a white, mild, open-textured cheese, is sometimes found in the form of Sage Derby, a variety with the white cheese layered or mottled with green coloured cheese that is flavoured with sage. Lancashire cheese is white and crumbly, excellent for toasting or sprinkling over soups. Leicester is a bright orange coloured cheese, with a creamy and tangy flavour and is very good for adding colour to cheese dishes, particularly in Welsh rarebit and cheese sauces.

Dunlop is one of the Scottish cheeses, although it is said to have been originally Irish, introduced during the seventeenth century by a fugitive from religious persecution. It is similar in texture to Cheddar but milder in flavour.

Denmark produces several copies of foreign cheeses, such as Brie, Camembert, Emmenthal and Gorgonzola, but the best-known of its original cheeses are Danish Blue, a blue-veined, salty but creamy cheese, Samsoe which has a slightly sweet flavour and Havarti which is a mild cheese.

Of the Dutch cheeses the best-known are Gouda and Edam. Gouda is strong, with a few small holes and a yellow rind. It is wheel-shaped, while Edam is round with a red skin when the cheese is exported.

Emmenthal and Gruyère are the best-known of the Swiss cheeses, and are both used in cookery, particularly in the making of *fondue*, the traditional Swiss dish of melted cheese (see page 50 for the recipe). Emmenthal has large holes and is creamy in taste while Gruyère has smaller holes and is tangier in flavour. A third well-known Swiss cheese is Appenzeller, a firm cheese with a spicy flavour and tiny holes.

France produces the widest range of cheeses in the world — nearly every village has its own speciality — of every shape, taste and texture. One of the most popular is Camembert, a pale yellow cheese of soft, creamy texture which originated in Normandy. Its rind is orange-yellow with a powdery white crust. Next in popularity is Brie, very similar to Camembert in texture, but with its own distinctive flavour.

Roquefort, a salty cheese made from ewes' milk, has a greyish crust and is flecked inside with green-blue, from the action of a mould similar to penicillin which is found in the caves where the cheese is stored.

Port Salut was originally made by Trappist monks, and is a semi-hard cheese, mild and fresh in flavour and in texture rather like butter. It is one of the best all round French cheeses. Fromage au Marc de Raisin is a sweet, cream cheese rolled in a crust of grape seeds. These are only a very few of the 400 to 500 cheeses of France, most of which are local specialities.

Cheese is a fundamental ingredient in Italian cooking, and may be classified according to its use — grating, cooking and for the table.

The hard Italian cheeses, used mostly in their grated form, are Parmigiano Reggiano, the original Parmesan, and Pecorino Romano, a sharp cheese made from fresh ewes' milk.

The most important cooking cheese in northern Italy is *grana*, of which Parmesan is the best-known variety. In the south, Mozzarella is the chief cooking cheese, very often used in pizzas. Mozzarella is ideally made from buffalo milk but most often from cows' milk. Ricotta is a fresh, moist, unsalted cottage cheese much used in Italian cooking and is the traditional ingredient in classic Italian cheesecake.

Of the eating cheeses, the best-known are Gorgonzola and Bel Paese. Gorgonzola is a blue-veined cheese, spiced and sharp in flavour. Bel Paese is rubbery, mild and soft.

USES FOR CHEESE
Cheese is one of the most versatile of foods, and can be eaten both cooked and uncooked, depending on the variety in question. Serve it, for instance, as a snack with milk for children, as a savoury course at the end of a special meal, or with French bread and butter, as the delicious adjunct to a wine party! Its cooking uses are equally numerous: it may be served in soups, savoury dishes (particularly Italian pasta sauces), and in desserts.

TYPES OF CHEESE FOR COOKING
Wherever cheeses are produced, they can generally be classified under three types: cream, soft and hard. All cheeses are suitable for eating on their own and some are more suitable for use in cooking than others.

Soft and semi-soft cheeses can be used in cooking but tend to be sticky. Hard cheeses — Cheddar, Edam, Gruyère, Emmenthal, Cheshire, Parmesan, Lancashire, Leicester and Derby — are ideal for cookery. Very hard cheeses, such as Parmesan and Pecorino are generally grated before using.

Whatever type of cheese is used in cooking, it should never receive more heat than is necessary to melt and if necessary brown it, because overcooking makes it tough and indigestible. When cheese is being grated prior to cooking, a fine grater should be used for hard cheese, while a soft cheese should be shredded. Very soft cheese can simply be sliced thinly.

STORING CHEESE
Once cut, cheese deteriorates fairly rapidly, and it is advisable to buy only enough for a few days or for a week at most, and to store it in a cool place, such as a cold larder. It should be covered loosely, but not so as to make it airtight. If it is airtight it may become mouldy, while if it is entirely exposed to the air it will become hard and dry. Cheese can be stored in the refrigerator for about one week but should be wrapped in waxed paper or aluminium foil, otherwise it will dry too rapidly.

Cheese can be hardened and dried by hanging it in a cheesecloth bag where the air can circulate around it. Dried, grated cheese can be stored in a screw-top jar for several weeks. If you have a home freezer, freshly grated cheese, packed in polythene bags, is a useful standby to have to add to pasta sauces and savoury dishes.

Cheese Bakes

☆ ① ① ◫

Easy and quick to prepare, Cheese Bakes make a tasty first course, or a light lunch dish.

2-4 SERVINGS

1 oz. [2 tablespoons] butter
4 oz. mushrooms, wiped clean and sliced
10 fl. oz. double cream [1¼ cups heavy cream], whipped until thick
4 oz. [1 cup] Cheddar cheese, grated
¼ teaspoon grated nutmeg
½ teaspoon salt
¼ teaspoon black pepper
8 oz. cooked smoked haddock, skinned, boned and flaked

Preheat the oven to fairly hot 375°F (Gas Mark 5, 190°C). Using half of the butter, grease 4 ramekins, individual baking dishes or one medium-sized baking dish, and set aside.

In a small saucepan, melt the remaining butter over moderate heat. When the foam subsides, add the mushrooms and cook, stirring occasionally, for 5 minutes.

Remove the pan from the heat and drain the mushrooms, discarding the juice. Set the mushrooms aside.

In a medium-sized mixing bowl, combine the whipped cream, half of the cheese, the nutmeg, salt and pepper. Stir in the haddock and mushrooms.

Pour equal amounts of the mixture into the ramekins or baking dish. Sprinkle over the remaining cheese.

Place the dishes or dish in the oven and bake for 20 to 30 minutes, or until the tops are lightly browned.

Remove the dishes or dish from the oven and serve immediately.

Cheese and Bread Bake

☆ ① ◫

This savoury bake makes a light and tasty supper dish, and is delicious garnished with crisply fried bacon and parsley.

4 SERVINGS

1 thick slice white bread, cubed
7 fl. oz. [⅞ cup] milk
8 slices of white bread, crusts removed
1½ oz. [3 tablespoons] butter
3 eggs, separated
1½ tablespoons flour
8 oz. [2 cups] Cheddar cheese, grated

Garnish this delicious Cheese and Bread Bake with bacon and parsley, as here, and serve as a filling lunch or supper dish.

½ teaspoon salt
¼ teaspoon grated nutmeg
4 fl. oz. single cream [½ cup light cream]

Preheat the oven to moderate 350°F (Gas Mark 4, 180°C).

Put the bread cubes in a shallow dish and sprinkle over half of the milk. In another dish, spread out the bread slices and sprinkle them with the remaining milk. Leave the cubes and slices to soak.

In a large bowl, cream the butter with a wooden spoon and mix in the egg yolks, one at a time. Stir in the flour. Add the soaked bread cubes, cheese, salt and nutmeg. Blend well and stir in the cream.

In a medium-sized bowl, beat the egg whites with a wire whisk until they are stiff. Fold them into the cheese mixture.

Line a greased straight-sided, oven-proof dish or casserole with the soaked bread slices. Pour the cheese mixture into the dish. Bake in the oven for 35 to 40 minutes. Serve immediately.

Beef and Cheese Roll

Served with a green vegetable and buttered noodles, this is a tasty and easy-to-prepare main dish for a family lunch or supper. The tomato sauce is served separately and may be made a day or two in advance, stored in the refrigerator in a covered jar, and reheated before serving.

4 SERVINGS

3 thick slices white bread, crusts removed
4 tablespoons milk
1½ lb. minced [ground] beef
2 eggs, lightly beaten
2 teaspoons dry mustard
1 teaspoon salt
⅛ teaspoon black pepper
½ teaspoon dried basil
1 onion, finely chopped
2 tablespoons finely chopped fresh parsley
1 tablespoon flour
8 oz. Mozzarella cheese, thinly sliced
1 oz. [2 tablespoons] butter, melted
SAUCE
1½ oz. [3 tablespoons] butter
2 medium-sized onions, finely chopped
1 garlic clove, crushed
1 lb. ripe tomatoes, blanched, peeled and chopped
1 teaspoon dried thyme
⅛ teaspoon salt
2 fl. oz. [¼ cup] red wine
⅛ teaspoon black pepper

Put the bread into a large bowl and pour the milk over it. Gently squeeze the bread and pour off the excess milk. Add the meat, eggs, mustard, salt, pepper, basil, onion and parsley. With your hands, knead the ingredients together until they are thoroughly blended.

Lightly dust a piece of waxed paper or aluminium foil with the flour. Put the meat mixture on it. With floured hands, press the meat into a thin rectangle. Cover lightly with aluminium foil and place the meat in the refrigerator for 1 hour or until it is thoroughly chilled.

Preheat the oven to moderate 350°F (Gas Mark 4, 180°C).

When the meat is cold, cover the top of it evenly with the sliced cheese.

Roll the meat, beginning at a narrow end, using the paper to lift it.

Place the beef roll carefully in a shallow baking tin, with the joined edges underneath. Brush the meat with the melted butter. Bake in the oven for 50 minutes.

Meanwhile, make the tomato sauce. In a medium-sized saucepan, melt the butter

Beef and Cheese Roll is creamy slices of Mozzarella cheese enclosed by a minced [ground] beef mixture.

over moderate heat. When the foam subsides, add the onions and garlic and fry, stirring occasionally, for 5 to 7 minutes or until the onions are soft and translucent but not brown.

Add the tomatoes, thyme, salt, red wine and pepper, and reduce the heat to low. Simmer the sauce for 40 minutes, stirring occasionally. Pour into a warmed sauceboat and serve with the beef roll.

Crowdie

This traditional Scottish cheese takes only a few hours to prepare, and can be varied by mixing it with chopped nuts, herbs or other seasonings.

4 SERVINGS

2 pints [5 cups] unpasteurized milk, fresh or sour
½ teaspoon rennet
1 tablespoon single [light] cream
½ teaspoon salt
½ teaspoon white pepper

Pour the milk into a medium-sized saucepan. Place the pan over moderate heat and heat the milk to blood heat. Remove the pan from the heat and pour the milk into a large bowl. Stir in the rennet. Set the bowl aside in a warm place for 10 minutes or until the milk separates into curds and whey.

Line a colander with two or three layers of cheesecloth or muslin and place it over a large bowl. Pour the curds and whey into the colander. Leave the curds to drain for 1½ to 2 hours. When the whey no longer drains out, turn the curds into a medium-sized serving bowl. Discard the whey.

With a wooden spoon, stir the cream, salt and pepper into the curds. Mix to a smooth consistency. Taste the crowdie and add more seasoning if desired. Leave in a cool place until it is set.

Devilled Cheese

A variant on Welsh Rarebit, Devilled Cheese makes an excellent quick and tasty supper dish.

6 SERVINGS

8 oz. [2 cups] Cheddar cheese, finely grated
4 teaspoons chutney
3 teaspoons curry powder
6 slices white bread, toasted, buttered and kept hot

Preheat the grill [broiler] to moderately high.

In a medium-sized mixing bowl, mix the cheese, chutney and curry powder together with a fork. With a knife, spread the mixture on one side of each slice of toast. Place the toast on the grill [broiler] rack and grill [broil] for 4 minutes or until the mixture is bubbling.

Remove the toast from the heat and serve at once.

Glamorgan Sausages

A marvellous family lunch or supper dish, Glamorgan Sausages are made from a tasty and economical mixture of cheese, onion and herbs. Accompany with French fried potatoes and peas.

2 SERVINGS

1 large onion, finely chopped
3 oz. [¾ cup] Cheddar cheese, finely grated
2 oz. [1 cup] fresh white breadcrumbs
1 tablespoon finely chopped fresh parsley
½ teaspoon dried thyme
1 teaspoon salt
½ teaspoon black pepper
¼ teaspoon dry mustard
1 egg yolk
2 tablespoons flour
1 egg white, lightly beaten
3 oz. [1 cup] dry white breadcrumbs
2 oz. [¼ cup] butter
2 tablespoons vegetable oil

In a medium-sized mixing bowl, combine the onion, cheese, fresh breadcrumbs, parsley, thyme, salt, pepper, mustard and egg yolk with a fork.

With your hands, shape the mixture into eight sausages. Dip each sausage in the flour, then in the egg white and then roll it in the dry breadcrumbs.

In a large frying-pan, melt the butter with the oil over moderate heat. When the foam subsides, add the sausages and fry, turning occasionally, for 5 to 8 minutes, or until they are well browned on all sides.

Remove the pan from the heat and transfer the sausages to a warmed serving dish. Serve at once.

Gougère
CHEESE PASTRY

A classic French pastry, said to have originated at Sens, Gougère may be served hot or cold, as an hors d'oeuvre or a delicious light lunch or supper dish.

4 SERVINGS

4 oz. [½ cup] plus 1 teaspoon butter
8 fl. oz. [1 cup] water
1 teaspoon salt
6 oz. [1½ cups] flour
4 eggs

Glamorgan Sausages — inexpensive and traditionally Welsh.

4 oz. Gruyère cheese, finely diced

Preheat the oven to hot 425°F (Gas Mark 7, 220°C).

Using the teaspoon of butter, lightly grease a large baking sheet. Set aside.

Put the remaining butter, the water and salt in a large saucepan. Place the pan over moderate heat and cook, stirring frequently, until the butter has melted and the mixture comes to the boil.

Remove the pan from the heat and stir in the flour. Return the pan to the heat and cook, stirring constantly, for 3 to 4 minutes, or until the mixture forms a dough and comes away easily from the sides of the pan.

Remove the pan from the heat and beat in the eggs, one at a time. Then beat in all but 2 tablespoons of the cheese.

Place heaped tablespoonfuls of the mixture, one against the other, in the shape of a ring, on the greased baking sheet.

Sprinkle the remaining cheese over the top of the dough ring and place it in the oven.

Bake for 40 to 45 minutes, or until the gougère is puffed and brown.

Remove from the oven and serve immediately or allow to cool before serving.

Cottage Cheese and Grapefruit Cups

This dish makes either a refreshing (and slimming!) first course or, served with crispbread and fresh fruit, a tasty light lunch.

4 SERVINGS

2 large grapefruit, halved
8 lettuce leaves, washed
12 oz. cottage cheese
4-inch piece of cucumber, cut into cubes

With a sharp knife, carefully cut around the grapefruit halves between the skin and flesh. Remove the flesh, discarding membrane and pith, and chop into bite-sized pieces.

Line each grapefruit shell with two lettuce leaves.

In a mixing bowl, combine the cottage cheese, cucumber and grapefruit flesh, beating to mix well. Pile the mixture back into the shells and serve at once.

Cheese and Ham Rolls

Cheese and Ham Rolls may either be served as a light luncheon, accompanied by new potatoes and French beans or, in greater quantities, as part of a buffet table at a party.

2 SERVINGS

4 oz. [½ cup] ricotta cheese
2 tablespoons mayonnaise
2 tablespoons chopped walnuts
1 celery stalk, trimmed and finely chopped
¼ teaspoon salt
¼ teaspoon black pepper
4 thin slices Gruyère cheese, about 4- x 6-inches
4 thin slices cooked ham
1 teaspoon prepared French mustard

Place the ricotta cheese, mayonnaise, walnuts, chopped celery, salt and pepper in a medium-sized mixing bowl. Using a wooden spoon, mix all the ingredients together until they are well blended. Set the bowl aside.

Place the slices of cheese on a flat working surface and lay the ham slices on top of them. Spread the mustard thinly over the ham. Spoon a quarter of the ricotta cheese mixture on to each slice of ham. Carefully roll the ham and

Cottage Cheese and Grapefruit Cup - a perfectly delicious lunch for would-be slimmers!

cheese up around the cheese mixture to form a cylinder and secure with cocktail sticks.

Place the rolls on a serving plate and serve immediately.

Mozzarella Chicken

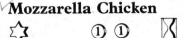

Delightfully different, Mozzarella Chicken makes a delicious family dinner dish. Serve it with plain boiled rice and a crisp salad.

6 SERVINGS

2 tablespoons vegetable oil
1 medium-sized onion, finely chopped
14 oz. canned peeled tomatoes
2 tablespoons tomato purée
1 teaspoon dried oregano
1 teaspoon salt
½ teaspoon black pepper
6 streaky bacon slices
1 oz. [2 tablespoons] butter
1 teaspoon finely chopped fresh tarragon
6 chicken breasts, skinned and boned
4 oz. Mozzarella cheese, cut into slices

In a medium-sized saucepan, heat the oil over moderate heat. When the oil is hot, add the onion and fry, stirring occasionally, for 5 to 7 minutes, or until it is soft and translucent but not brown.

Add the tomatoes with the can juice, the tomato purée, oregano, salt and pepper. Stir well and bring the liquid to the boil over high heat. Reduce the heat to very low and simmer the tomato sauce for 20 minutes, stirring occasionally.

Meanwhile, in a large frying-pan, fry the bacon over moderate heat for 5 minutes or until it is crisp and has rendered most of its fat. Remove the bacon from the pan and set aside to drain on kitchen paper towels. Keep warm.

Add the butter to the bacon fat in the frying-pan. When the foam subsides, stir in the tarragon. Add the chicken breasts and fry, turning occasionally, for 15 to 20 minutes, or until they are tender.

Preheat the grill [broiler] to high.

Remove the frying-pan from the heat. With a slotted spoon, transfer the chicken breasts to a warmed flameproof serving dish. Place a slice of bacon over each breast and pour over the tomato sauce.

Place the slices of cheese over the top and place the dish under the grill [broiler]. Grill [broil] for 4 to 5 minutes or until the cheese has melted and is lightly browned.

Remove the dish from the heat and serve at once, straight from the dish.

Cheese and Onion Pie

This economical pie can be served as a light supper dish with a mixed salad.

4 SERVINGS

8 oz. [2 cups] flour
1 teaspoon salt
2 oz. [¼ cup] plus 3 tablespoons butter
2 oz. [¼ cup] vegetable fat
2 tablespoons iced water
3 onions, finely chopped
2 garlic cloves, crushed
8 oz. [2 cups] Cheddar cheese, grated
1 egg, lightly beaten
½ teaspoon white pepper

Make the pastry by sifting the flour and half the salt into a mixing bowl. Put in 2 ounces [¼ cup] of the butter and the vegetable fat and cut it into small pieces with a table knife. With your fingertips, rub the fat into the flour until the mixture resembles fine breadcrumbs. Add 2 tablespoons of iced water and, using the knife, mix it into the flour. With your hands, mix until a smooth dough is formed. Add more water if the dough is too dry. Form the dough into a ball and wrap it in greaseproof or waxed paper. Chill for 20 minutes.

Preheat the oven to fairly hot 400°F (Gas Mark 6, 200°C). Grease a medium-sized pie dish with 1 tablespoon of the remaining butter and set it aside.

In a frying-pan, melt the remaining 2 tablespoons of butter over moderate heat. Add the chopped onions and garlic, reduce the heat to low and cook the mixture gently for 10 minutes, stirring occasionally. Set aside.

In a mixing bowl, combine the onion mixture with the grated cheese. Add most of the beaten egg (keep a little to glaze the pie crust), remaining salt and the pepper and beat to blend well. Set aside.

Divide the dough ball into two portions, one slightly larger than the other. Roll out the larger portion of dough until it is quite thin and is large enough to overlap the sides of the pie dish. Line the pie dish, and trim off the excess dough with a knife. Spoon the cheese-and-onion mixture into the dish.

Roll out the other portion of dough to a circle slightly larger than the pie dish. Place the circle of dough on top of the filling. Fold under the overhanging dough and press the edges together with your fingertips to seal. Coat the surface of the pie with the remaining beaten egg. Bake in the centre of the oven for about 35 minutes, or until the pastry is deep golden. Serve either hot or cold.

Neapolitan Pizzas

A traditional Italian dish from Naples, Neapolitan Pizzas make a delicious meal, which is both inexpensive and filling. Serve Neapolitan Pizzas with a crisp green salad and a bottle of dry white Italian wine.

2 SERVINGS

½ oz. fresh yeast
¼ teaspoon sugar
4 fl. oz. [½ cup] plus 1 tablespoon
    lukewarm water
8 oz. [2 cups] flour
1 teaspoon salt
2 teaspoons olive oil

FILLING

2 tablespoons tomato purée
4 medium-sized tomatoes,
    blanched, peeled, seeded and
    coarsely chopped
8 oz. Mozzarella cheese, sliced
8 anchovy fillets, cut in half
¼ teaspoon black pepper
2 teaspoons chopped fresh oregano

Crumble the yeast into a small bowl. Add the sugar and 1 tablespoon of the water and cream the water and yeast together. Set the bowl aside in a warm, draught-free place for 15 to 20 minutes, or until the yeast mixture is puffed up and frothy.

Sift the flour and salt into a warmed,

Crisp pastry topped with tomatoes, anchovies and Mozzarella cheese - that's Neapolitan Pizzas. Serve with mellow red wine.

large mixing bowl. Make a well in the centre and pour in the yeast mixture and the remaining water.

Using your fingers or a spatula, gradually draw the flour into the liquids. Continue mixing until all the flour is incorporated and the dough comes away from the sides of the bowl.

Turn the dough out on to a lightly floured board or marble slab and knead it for about 10 minutes, reflouring the surface if the dough becomes sticky. The dough should be elastic and smooth.

Rinse, thoroughly dry and lightly grease the large mixing bowl. Shape the dough into a ball and return it to the bowl. Dust the top of the dough with a little flour and cover the bowl with a clean, damp cloth. Set the bowl in a warm, draught-free place and leave it for 45 minutes to 1 hour, or until the dough has risen and has almost doubled in bulk.

Preheat the oven to very hot 450°F (Gas Mark 8, 230°C). With a teaspoon of the olive oil, lightly grease a large baking sheet and set aside.

Turn the risen dough out of the bowl

on to a floured surface and knead it for 3 minutes. Cut the dough in half. With a lightly floured rolling pin, roll out each dough half to a circle about ¼-inch thick. Carefully arrange the dough circles, well apart, on the prepared baking sheet.

Spoon a tablespoon of tomato purée on to each circle and spread it out with a table knife. Decorate each circle with half of the tomatoes, cheese and anchovy fillets and sprinkle over the black pepper and oregano. Moisten each pizza with the remaining olive oil.

Place the pizzas in the centre of the oven and bake for 15 to 20 minutes, or until the dough is cooked and the cheese has melted. Remove from the oven and transfer the pizzas to a warmed serving dish. Serve immediately.

Gruyère Puffs

These light and savoury puffs are a favourite for children's tea-parties.

4 SERVINGS

2 egg whites
4 oz. [1 cup] Gruyère cheese, grated
2 oz. [⅔ cup] fine dry white
    breadcrumbs
    sufficient vegetable oil for
    deep-frying

In a medium-sized mixing bowl, beat the egg whites with a wire whisk or rotary beater until they are frothy. Add the grated cheese and, with your fingers, work the mixture into a soft paste. Form the paste into small balls by rolling teaspoonfuls between the palms of your hands.

Sprinkle the breadcrumbs on to a sheet of greaseproof or waxed paper. Roll each ball in the breadcrumbs so that they are coated on all sides.

Place the crumbed cheese balls on a plate and put them in the refrigerator to chill for 2½ hours.

Fill a large deep-frying pan one-third full with vegetable oil. Place the pan over moderate heat and heat the oil until it reaches 350°F on a deep-fat thermometer, or until a cube of stale bread dropped into the oil turns golden in 55 seconds.

Carefully drop a few of the balls into the oil and cook them for 2 minutes, or until they are puffed and lightly browned. With a slotted spoon, transfer the balls to kitchen paper towels to drain. Keep them warm while you fry the remaining balls in the same way.

Serve hot.

Grated Cheddar cheese and fish combine to make Cheese and Sardine Fritters a wholesome yet inexpensive supper dish for the family.

Cheese and Sardine Fritters

☆   ①   🔪

Cheese and Sardine Fritters may be served with sweet potatoes, lots of mixed, tossed salad and some ice-cold lager.

4 SERVINGS

2 lb. fresh sardines, cleaned and with the eyes removed
10 oz. [2½ cups] Cheddar cheese, grated
½ garlic clove, crushed
2 eggs, lightly beaten
juice of 1 lime
6 oz. [1½ cups] flour
½ teaspoon freshly ground black pepper
2 oz. [⅔ cup] fine dry white breadcrumbs
sufficient vegetable oil for deep-frying
3 limes, quartered

Preheat the grill [broiler] to moderately high.

Wash the sardines under cold running water and pat them dry with kitchen paper towels.

Place the sardines on the rack in the grill [broiler] pan and place the pan under the grill [broiler]. Grill [broil] for 6 minutes, turning the fish occasionally. Remove the grill [broiler] pan from the heat.

Place the sardines on a flat surface. Remove and discard the head, tail and spine from each sardine. Place the flesh in a medium-sized mixing bowl. Add the cheese, garlic, 1 egg and the lime juice. Using a wooden spoon, blend the mixture well.

On a plate, combine the flour, pepper and the breadcrumbs. Place the remaining egg on a second plate.

Roll the sardine mixture into small patties and dip each patty first in the beaten egg, then in the flour mixture, coating them thoroughly and shaking off any excess.

Fill a large deep-frying pan one-third full with vegetable oil. Set the pan over moderate heat and heat the oil until it registers 375°F on a deep-fat thermometer or until a small cube of stale bread dropped into the oil turns golden brown in 40 seconds. Place the patties, a few at a time, in a deep-frying basket and carefully lower the basket into the vegetable oil. Fry the patties for 3 to 5 minutes or until they are golden brown all over. Remove the basket from the oil and transfer the fritters to kitchen paper towels to drain. Keep warm while you fry and drain the remaining patties in the same way.

Place the fritters on a heated serving dish, garnish with the lime quarters and serve immediately.

Cheese Soufflé

☆ ① ⧗

Serve Cheese Soufflé with a crisp green salad, or a green vegetable such as courgettes [zucchini], and French bread.

6-8 SERVINGS

2 oz. [¼ cup] plus 1 tablespoon butter
5 oz. [1¼ cups] cheese, coarsely grated (preferably a mixture of Gruyère and Parmesan)
4 tablespoons flour
10 fl. oz. [1¼ cups] milk, scalded
1 teaspoon salt
⅛ teaspoon white pepper
⅛ teaspoon ground mace
⅛ teaspoon paprika

5 egg yolks
6 egg whites
¼ teaspoon cream of tartar

Preheat the oven to moderate 350°F (Gas Mark 4, 180°C).

With the tablespoon of butter, grease a 2½-pint [1½-quart] soufflé dish. Sprinkle 4 tablespoons of the grated cheese around the inside of the dish and, with a table knife, press it on to the bottom and sides. Set the soufflé dish aside.

In a large saucepan, melt the remaining butter over moderate heat. With a wooden spoon, stir the flour into the butter and cook, stirring constantly, for 1 minute. Do not let this roux brown.

Remove the pan from the heat. Grad-

Elegant to look at, easy to prepare and super to eat - that's creamy Cheese Soufflé!

ually add the milk, stirring constantly.

Return the pan to the heat and cook the mixture, stirring constantly, for 1 minute or until it is thick and smooth.

Remove the pan from the heat and add ½ teaspoon salt, the pepper, mace and paprika. Beat the egg yolks, a little at a time, into the hot sauce. Set the pan aside to allow the egg yolk mixture to cool slightly.

In a mixing bowl, beat the egg whites with a rotary beater or wire whisk until they are foamy. Add the remaining salt and the cream of tartar. Continue beating until the egg whites form stiff peaks.

Stir the remaining cheese into the hot sauce. When the cheese is thoroughly mixed in, spoon the egg whites on top of the sauce and gently, but quickly, fold them in with a metal spoon.

Spoon the mixture into the prepared soufflé dish. With a table knife, carefully mark a deep circle in the centre of the soufflé.

Place the soufflé in the centre of the oven and bake for 40 to 45 minutes, or until it is lightly browned on top and it has risen ½-inch above the top of the dish.

Remove the soufflé dish from the oven and serve at once.

Cheese Soup

☆ ① ⋈

This unusual and warming winter soup is especially good with hot crusty bread and lots of butter.

4 SERVINGS

2 oz. [¼ cup] butter
2 medium-sized onions, chopped
2 tablespoons flour
4 fl. oz. [½ cup] chicken stock
1½ pints [3¾ cups] milk
12 oz. [3 cups] Cheddar cheese, grated
3 oz. [¾ cup] Gruyère cheese, grated
½ teaspoon prepared mustard
½ teaspoon salt
¼ teaspoon black pepper
1½ teaspoons paprika
1 teaspoon Worcestershire sauce

In a large heavy saucepan, melt the butter over moderate heat. When the foam subsides, add the onions and cook for 8 to 10 minutes or until they are golden. Stir in the flour and cook, stirring, for 2 to 3 minutes. Remove the pan from the heat and gradually stir in the stock. When the mixture is smooth, stir in the milk.

Add the cheese and the mustard. Return the pan to low heat. Cook, stirring, until the cheese melts. Do not allow the soup to reach boiling point. Remove the pan from the heat. Season with salt, pepper and paprika. The amount of seasoning depends on the strength of the cheese, and it is advisable to taste and season as the soup requires. Add the Worcestershire sauce and serve.

Tuna Cheese with Dill ✓

☆ ① ⋈

This delicious dish makes a perfect, inexpensive supper dish for the family. Serve with baked potatoes and some salad.

The ideal snack meal, Tuna Cheese with Dill can be made from the contents of your store cupboard.

4 SERVINGS

1½ oz. [3 tablespoons] butter
1 medium-sized onion, finely chopped
10 oz. condensed cream of mushroom soup
½ teaspoon white pepper
¼ teaspoon salt
1 teaspoon dried dill
10 oz. canned tuna fish, drained and flaked
4 oz. canned sweetcorn, drained
3 oz. [¾ cup] Gruyère cheese, grated
6 thin slices of Gruyère cheese
1½ oz. [¾ cup] fresh breadcrumbs

Preheat the grill [broiler] to moderately high.

In a medium-sized frying-pan, melt the butter over moderate heat. When the foam subsides, add the onion and fry, stirring occasionally, for 5 to 7 minutes or until it is soft and translucent but not brown.

Stir in the soup, pepper, salt and dill and mix well. Bring the mixture to the boil. Stir in the tuna fish, sweetcorn and half of the grated cheese. Heat the mixture, stirring occasionally, for 3 minutes or until it is heated through.

Remove the pan from the heat and spoon the mixture into a medium-sized baking dish. Lay the cheese slices over the mixture.

In a small bowl, combine the remaining grated cheese and the breadcrumbs. Sprinkle them over the cheese slices, to cover completely.

Place the dish under the grill [broiler] and grill [broil] for 5 to 8 minutes or until the top is brown and bubbly. Remove the dish from the heat and serve at once.

Asparagus Quiche

A delicately flavoured and coloured dish, Asparagus Quiche may be served with a lettuce salad.

4-6 SERVINGS

1 x 9-inch flan case made with shortcrust pastry

FILLING

6 oz. lean cooked ham, chopped

4 fl. oz. single cream [½ cup light cream]

3 fl. oz. [⅜ cup] milk

3 eggs

1 oz. [¼ cup] Cheddar cheese, grated

¼ teaspoon salt

½ teaspoon white pepper

12 asparagus tips, cooked and drained

Preheat the oven to fairly hot 400°F (Gas Mark 6, 200°C). Place the flan case on a baking sheet.

Cover the bottom of the flan case with the chopped ham and set aside.

In a medium-sized mixing bowl, combine the cream, milk, eggs, grated cheese, salt and pepper and beat well to blend.

Pour the mixture over the ham. Arrange the asparagus tips around the edge of the filling.

The perfect dish for impressive entertaining - Asparagus Quiche.

Place the baking sheet in the centre of the oven. Bake the quiche for 35 to 40 minutes or until the filling is set and firm and golden brown on top.

Remove the baking sheet from the oven and serve the quiche at once, if you are serving it hot.

Quiche Lorraine

CHEESE AND BACON QUICHE

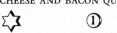

Quiche Lorraine makes a beautifully elegant light lunch or supper dish served with a tossed mixed salad and crusty bread. There are, by the way, almost as many 'original' recipes for this dish as

there are villages in Lorraine — this is merely one of the basic ones and lays no claim to being the one true version !

4-6 SERVINGS

1 x 9-inch flan case made with shortcrust pastry

FILLING

4 oz. Gruyère cheese, thinly sliced

6 oz. lean bacon, grilled [broiled] until crisp and crumbled

5 fl. oz. single cream [⅝ cup light cream]

3 eggs

½ teaspoon salt

½ teaspoon white pepper

Preheat the oven to fairly hot 400°F (Gas Mark 6, 200°C). Place the flan case on a baking sheet.

Cover the bottom of the flan case with the cheese slices, then cover with the crumbled bacon. Set aside.

In a bowl, combine the cream, eggs, salt and pepper and beat well to blend. Pour the mixture over the cheese.

Place the baking sheet in the centre of the oven and bake the quiche for 25 to 30 minutes or until the filling is set and firm and golden brown on top.

Remove the baking sheet from the oven and serve the quiche at once, if you are serving it hot.

Mushroom Quiche

☆ ① ✕

A ·marvellously tasty dish, Mushroom Quiche may be served either hot or cold.

4-6 SERVINGS

1 x 9-inch flan case made with shortcrust pastry

FILLING

2 oz. [¼ cup] butter

2 shallots, finely chopped

1 lb. button mushrooms, wiped clean and thinly sliced

¼ teaspoon salt

¼ teaspoon white pepper

¼ teaspoon grated nutmeg

4 fl. oz. single cream [½ cup light cream]

3 eggs

2 oz. [½ cup] Cheddar cheese, grated

Preheat the oven to fairly hot 400°F (Gas Mark 6, 200°C). Place the flan case on a baking sheet and set aside.

In a large frying-pan, melt the butter over moderate heat. When the foam subsides, add the shallots and cook, stirring occasionally, for 3 to 4 minutes or until they are soft and translucent — but not brown. Add the mushrooms to the pan and cook, stirring occasionally, for 3

minutes. Remove the pan from the heat and stir in the salt, pepper and nutmeg.

In a medium-sized mixing bowl, combine the cream, eggs and grated cheese and beat well to blend.

Add the mixture to the mushrooms, stirring until they are blended.

Pour the mixture into the flan case and place the baking sheet in the centre of the oven. Bake the quiche for 25 to 30 minutes or until the filling is set and firm and golden brown on top.

Remove the baking sheet from the oven and serve the quiche at once, if you are serving it hot.

Three-Cheese Quiche

☆ ① ① ✕

A subtle mixture of Roquefort, Camembert and cream cheese gives a special rich taste to Three-Cheese Quiche. Serve as an elegant first course to a dinner or, with lots of salad and crusty bread, as a light lunch or supper. Served cold, this quiche makes an excellent picnic food. Serve with a selection of salads.

4-6 SERVINGS

1 x 9-inch flan case made with shortcrust pastry

FILLING

3 oz. Roquefort cheese, crumbled

3 oz. Camembert cheese, rind removed

3 oz. cream cheese

1 tablespoon softened butter

1 shallot, finely chopped

2 fl. oz. single cream [¼ cup light cream]

3 eggs

¼ teaspoon salt

⅛ teaspoon white pepper

⅛ teaspoon cayenne pepper

Preheat the oven to fairly hot 400°F (Gas Mark 6, 200°C). Place the flan case on a baking sheet and set aside.

In a medium-sized mixing bowl, mash the Roquefort, Camembert, cream cheese and butter together with a fork until the mixture is smooth and the ingredients well blended. (If the mixture is a little lumpy, put the cheese through a strainer, lined with a piece of cheesecloth, pressing down hard with the back of a wooden spoon.)

Stir in the shallot and beat well to mix.

In a second medium-sized mixing bowl, combine the cream, eggs, salt, pepper and cayenne and beat well to blend.

Add the cream mixture to the cheese, stirring constantly until they are well blended.

Pour the mixture into the flan case and place the baking sheet in the centre of the oven. Bake the quiche for 30 to 35 minutes or until the filling is set and firm and golden brown on top.

Remove the baking sheet from the oven and serve the quiche at once, if you are serving it hot.

Tuna Fish Quiche

☆ ① ① ✕

A delightfully satisfying light lunch or supper dish, Tuna Fish Quiche may be served with tomato and green pepper salad.

4-6 SERVINGS

1 x 9-inch flan case made with shortcrust pastry

FILLING

1 oz. [2 tablespoons] butter

2 small onions, finely chopped

1 large garlic clove, crushed

2 tablespoons chopped pimientos

7 oz. canned tuna fish, drained and flaked

2 oz. [⅓ cup] stoned black olives

¼ teaspoon salt

¾ teaspoon black pepper

⅛ teaspoon cayenne pepper

4 fl. oz. single cream [½ cup light cream]

3 eggs

2 oz. [½ cup] Cheddar cheese, grated

Preheat the oven to fairly hot 400°F (Gas Mark 6, 200°C). Place the flan case on a baking sheet and set aside.

In a large frying-pan, melt the butter over moderate heat. When the foam subsides, add the onions and garlic and cook, stirring occasionally, for 5 to 7 minutes or until the onions are soft and translucent but not brown.

Stir in the pimientos, tuna fish, olives, salt, pepper and cayenne and mix well to blend. Reduce the heat to low and simmer the mixture, stirring occasionally, for 5 minutes or until the tuna fish is heated through. Remove the pan from the heat and set aside.

In a medium-sized mixing bowl, combine the cream, eggs and grated cheese and beat well to blend.

Add the cream mixture to the tuna fish, stirring constantly until they are well blended.

Pour the mixture into the flan case and place the baking sheet in the centre of the oven. Bake the quiche for 35 to 40 minutes or until the filling is set and firm and golden brown on top.

Remove the baking sheet from the oven and serve the quiche at once, if you are serving it hot.

Bean Rarebit

This delicious, easy-to-make dish is a typical snack from the Southwestern United States. Serve for a snack lunch or supper.

4 SERVINGS

- 1 oz. [2 tablespoons] butter
- 1 medium-sized onion, finely chopped
- 1 garlic clove, crushed
- 1 green pepper, white pith removed, seeded and finely chopped
- 14 oz. canned kidney beans, drained
- 14 oz. canned baked beans
- 4 tablespoons tomato ketchup
- 1 tablespoon Worcestershire sauce
- $\frac{1}{2}$ teaspoon salt
- 1 teaspoon black pepper
- 2 teaspoons mild chilli powder
- 6 oz. [1$\frac{1}{2}$ cups] Cheddar cheese, grated
- 4 large slices hot buttered toast

In a medium-sized frying-pan, melt the butter over moderate heat. When the foam subsides, add the onion, garlic and green pepper and fry, stirring occasionally, for 5 to 7 minutes or until the onion is soft and translucent but not brown. Stir in the kidney beans, baked beans with the can juice, ketchup, Worcestershire sauce, salt, pepper and chilli powder and stir well to mix. Cook the mixture, stirring occasionally, for a further 5 minutes.

Stir in the cheese and cook, stirring constantly, for a further 3 minutes or until the cheese has melted and the mixture is hot and thick.

Remove the pan from the heat. Place the toast slices on individual serving plates and spoon the bean mixture over them. Serve at once.

Bean Rarebit is a warming mixture of beans, cheese and spices on toast.

Sweetcorn Rarebit

Sweetcorn Rarebit makes a delightful snack lunch, accompanied by a tomato and lettuce salad.

4 SERVINGS

- 1 oz. [2 tablespoons] butter
- 1 small green pepper, white pith removed, seeded and finely chopped
- 1 medium-sized onion, finely chopped
- 4 eggs
- $\frac{1}{2}$ teaspoon salt
- $\frac{1}{2}$ teaspoon freshly ground black pepper
- 3 drops Tabasco sauce
- 4 tablespoons tomato purée
- 6 oz. canned sweetcorn, drained
- 8 oz. [2 cups] Cheddar cheese, grated
- 4 slices toast, crusts removed and kept hot

Welsh Rarebit, a satisfying mixture of cheese, flavourings and ale or beer on toast, is almost the British national snack dish!

the cheese has melted.

Remove the pan from the heat and divide the mixture among the slices of toast. Place the toast in the grill [broiler] pan and place the pan under the heat. Grill [broil] for 3 to 4 minutes or until the mixture is golden brown. Remove the pan from under the heat.

Transfer the toast slices to individual warmed plates and serve the rarebit immediately.

Yorkshire Rarebit

☆ ① ⧗

This is a northern version of the traditional Welsh Rarebit, and makes a very nourishing and tasty lunch or supper dish. Serve Yorkshire Rarebit with a mixed salad and grilled [broiled] mushrooms or fried tomatoes.

2 SERVINGS

1 tablespoon butter
1 tablespoon flour
2 tablespoons milk
2 tablespoons brown ale or dark beer
½ teaspoon prepared French mustard
¼ teaspoon salt
½ teaspoon freshly ground black pepper
4 oz. [1 cup] Cheddar cheese, grated
2 slices hot buttered toast
2 thick slices lean cooked ham
2 poached eggs, kept hot

Preheat the grill [broiler] to moderately high.

In a small saucepan, melt the butter over moderate heat. Remove the pan from the heat and, with a wooden spoon, stir in the flour to make a smooth paste. Gradually add the milk, brown ale or beer, mustard, salt and pepper, stirring constantly and being careful to avoid lumps. Return the pan to low heat and cook, stirring constantly, for 2 to 3 minutes or until the mixture is thick and smooth. Add the cheese to the mixture and cook, stirring constantly, for a further 2 minutes or until the cheese has completely melted.

Remove the pan from the heat and divide the mixture between the 2 slices of toast. Place a slice of ham on each slice and place the toast on the rack in the grill [broiler] pan. Place the pan under the heat and grill [broil] for 3 to 4 minutes or until the ham has turned golden brown. Remove the pan from under the heat. Place a poached egg on each slice of toast.

Place each slice on a plate and serve at once.

In a small frying-pan, melt the butter over moderate heat. When the foam subsides, add the green pepper and onion and fry, stirring occasionally, for 5 to 7 minutes or until the onion is soft and translucent but not brown.

Meanwhile, in a medium-sized mixing bowl, using a wire whisk or rotary beater, lightly beat together the eggs, salt, pepper and Tabasco sauce. Set aside.

Add the tomato purée, sweetcorn and grated cheese to the frying-pan and cook, stirring constantly, until the cheese has melted. Pour the beaten egg mixture into the pan and cook, stirring constantly, for 5 to 7 minutes or until the mixture thickens slightly. Remove the pan from the heat.

Place the slices of toast on warmed, individual serving plates and carefully spoon equal quantities of the mixture on to the toast. Serve immediately.

Welsh Rarebit

☆ ① ⧗

Welsh Rarebit is a quickly made traditional British dish, which is both tasty and satisfying. Serve with grilled [broiled] tomatoes and a green salad for a light luncheon or supper.

4 SERVINGS

1 tablespoon butter

1 tablespoon flour
2 tablespoons milk
2 fl. oz. [¼ cup] brown ale or dark beer
2 teaspoons Worcestershire sauce
1 teaspoon prepared English mustard
½ teaspoon salt
½ teaspoon freshly ground black pepper
8 oz. [2 cups] Cheddar cheese, grated
4 slices toast, buttered and kept hot

Preheat the grill [broiler] to moderately high.

In a medium-sized saucepan, melt the butter over moderate heat. Remove the pan from the heat and, with a wooden spoon, stir in the flour to make a smooth paste. Gradually add the milk, ale or beer, Worcestershire sauce, mustard, salt and pepper, stirring constantly. Return the pan to low heat and cook, stirring constantly, for 2 to 3 minutes or until the mixture is thick and smooth. Add the cheese to the mixture and cook, stirring constantly, for a further 1 minute or until

Georgian Cheese Bread

☆ ① ① ⊠ ⊠ ⊠

A savoury cheese bread from one of the southern republics of the U.S.S.R., Georgian Cheese Bread is so popular that small individual versions of the bread are made and sold by hawkers in the streets.

ONE 2-POUND LOAF

½ oz. fresh yeast
½ teaspoon sugar
4 to 5 fl. oz. [½ to ⅝ cup] lukewarm
  milk
1 lb. [4 cups] flour
1 teaspoon salt
3 oz. [⅜ cup] plus 1 teaspoon butter,
  melted

FILLING

1¼ lb. Caerphilly or any crumbly
  white cheese, crumbled
2 oz. [¼ cup] butter, softened
1 egg
1 egg yolk
1 teaspoon chopped fresh parsley

Crumble the yeast into a small bowl and mash in the sugar with a fork. Add 4 tablespoons of the milk and cream the milk and yeast together. Set the bowl aside in a warm, draught-free place for 15 to 20 minutes or until the yeast mixture is puffed up and frothy.

Sift the flour and salt into a warmed large mixing bowl. Make a well in the centre and pour in the yeast mixture, the remaining milk and 3 ounces [⅜ cup] of the butter. Using your fingers or a spatula, gradually draw the flour mixture into the liquids. Continue mixing until all the flour is incorporated and the dough comes away from the sides of the bowl.

Turn the dough out on to a lightly floured board or marble slab and knead it for 8 minutes, reflouring the surface if the dough becomes sticky. The dough should be elastic and smooth.

Rinse, thoroughly dry and lightly grease the large mixing bowl. Shape the dough into a ball and return it to the bowl. Cover the bowl with a clean damp cloth and set it in a warm, draught-free place. Leave it for 1 hour, or until the dough has risen and almost doubled in bulk.

Turn the risen dough out of the bowl on to a floured surface and knead it for about 3 minutes. Shape the dough into a ball and return it to the bowl. Cover and leave for 1 hour, or until it has risen and almost doubled in bulk.

Meanwhile, prepare the filling. In a medium-sized mixing bowl, mash the cheese, butter, egg, egg yolk and parsley together, beating until the ingredients are well blended. Place the bowl in the refrigerator and chill the mixture until it

is required.

With the remaining teaspoon of butter, lightly grease an 8-inch loose-bottomed cake tin and set it aside.

Turn the risen dough out of the bowl on to a floured surface and, with a rolling pin, roll it out into a circle, approximately 21 inches in diameter. Lift the dough circle carefully on the rolling pin and place it over the cake tin so that there is an even amount of dough hanging all around the tin. Gently ease the dough into the tin, leaving the excess dough hanging over the sides.

Remove the filling from the refrigerator and spoon it into the centre of the lined tin. With your fingers, draw the excess dough up and over the filling, pleating it into loose folds. Gather the dough in the centre and twist it into a small knob.

Set the dough aside in a warm, draught-free place for 20 minutes, or until the dough has risen and increased in bulk.

Meanwhile, preheat the oven to fairly hot 400°F (Gas Mark 6, 200°C).

Place the tin in the oven and bake the bread for 30 minutes. Reduce the oven temperature to moderate 350°F (Gas Mark 4, 180°C) and bake for a further 20 minutes, or until the bread is well risen and deep golden in colour.

Remove the bread from the oven and leave it to cool in the tin for 30 minutes. Remove the sides and place the bread, still on the base of the tin, on a wire rack to cool completely. Serve cold.

Broccoli with Cheese Sauce

☆ ① ① ⊠

This is a novel way to prepare broccoli. Serve it with steak, chicken or fish.

6 SERVINGS

1½ to 2 lb. broccoli, washed and
  trimmed
1 teaspoon salt

SAUCE

1 oz. [2 tablespoons] butter
4 tablespoons flour
10 fl. oz. [1¼ cups] milk
¼ teaspoon white pepper
2 oz. [½ cup] Parmesan cheese,
  grated
6 anchovies, chopped, plus 4
  anchovies for garnish

Break the broccoli flowerets into medium-sized clusters. Place them in a pan with the salt and about 10 fluid ounces [1¼ cups] of boiling water. Bring the water back to the boil over moderately high heat and cook the broccoli, uncovered, for 5 minutes. Then cover the pan and cook for 10 to 15 minutes more.

Fabulous Georgian Cheese Bread from the USSR.

While the broccoli is cooking, prepare the sauce. In a small saucepan, melt the butter over moderate heat. Stir in the flour with a wooden spoon. Cook for 1 minute, stirring constantly. Remove the pan from the heat and add the milk, a little at a time, stirring constantly. Return the pan to the heat and cook until the sauce is thick. Add the pepper, cheese and chopped anchovies and continue stirring until the cheese has melted.

Drain the broccoli in a colander and arrange it on a warmed serving dish. Pour the sauce over the broccoli, garnish with the remaining anchovies and serve at once.

Cheese Fondue

☆ ① ① ⊠

A wonderfully sociable dish that is ideal for informal entertaining, Cheese Fondue (pictured on page 1) is best served with a well-chilled dry white wine, such as Fendant or Neuchâtel. When the fondue is ready, it is eaten by spearing the bread pieces on a fondue fork or skewer and dipping it into the pot.

4 SERVINGS

1 garlic clove, cut in half
8 fl. oz. [1 cup] dry white wine
1 teaspoon lemon juice
8 oz. Gruyère cheese, cut into
  small cubes
8 oz. Emmenthal cheese, cut into
  small cubes
2 teaspoons cornflour [cornstarch],
  dissolved in 1 tablespoon wine
¼ teaspoon black pepper
⅛ teaspoon cayenne pepper
2 tablespoons kirsch
1 long thin French loaf (*baguette*),
  cut into quarters, lengthways,
  then into 1-inch slices, crosswise

Rub the garlic halves around a saucepan and discard. Pour the wine and lemon juice into the pan and place it over low heat. When the liquid is hot, add the cheese cubes and stir until they melt and the mixture is blended. Add the cornflour [cornstarch] mixture, pepper and cayenne and cook, stirring constantly, for 2 minutes, or until the mixture thickens. Do not allow to boil.

Stir in the kirsch and beat for 1 minute. Then pour the cheese mixture into the fondue pot. Light the spirit burner and place the fondue pot over the heat. The fondue is now ready to serve with the bread.

Mozzarella Savoury

☆ ① ① ✗ ✗

A simple dish to prepare and a filling one to eat, Mozzarella Savoury may be served with lots of green salad and a well-chilled white wine.

6 SERVINGS

2 oz. [¼ cup] butter
1 medium-sized onion, finely chopped
¼ teaspoon salt
¼ teaspoon black pepper
2 teaspoons dried basil
1 lb. tomatoes, blanched, peeled, seeded and chopped
2 oz. cream cheese
15 oz. [6 cups] cooked Italian rice
3 tablespoons olive oil
4 oz. [1 cup] Parmesan cheese, finely grated
6 x 4 oz. Mozzarella cheeses
12 black olives, stoned

In a medium-sized saucepan, melt the butter over moderate heat. When the foam subsides, add the onion and fry, stirring occasionally, for 5 to 7 minutes or until it is soft and translucent but not brown. Add the salt, pepper, 1 teaspoon of the basil and the tomatoes. Reduce the heat to low, cover the pan and simmer for 1 hour. Remove the pan from the heat and set aside to cool to room temperature.

Place the vegetable mixture in the jar of an electric blender and blend until the mixture forms a purée. Scrape the purée into a medium-sized mixing bowl. Add the cream cheese and beat the mixture until it is well blended.

Place the cooked rice, oil, the remaining basil and the Parmesan in a large mixing bowl. Stir well to mix.

Mozzarella Savoury is blend of cheese, rice, olives and sauce.

Spoon the rice mixture on to a large, flat serving dish. Pour half the purée mixture into the centre of the rice, and pour the remainder into a sauceboat. Place the Mozzarella cheeses down the centre of the dish and garnish with the olives.

Serve cold.

Cheese Pancakes

☆ ① ✗

Serve these light and tasty Cheese Pancakes with grilled [broiled] bacon and tomatoes for a delicious lunch.

4 SERVINGS

4 oz. [1 cup] flour
½ teaspoon salt
4 eggs
12 fl. oz. double cream [1½ cups heavy cream]
3 tablespoons vegetable oil

Classic Quenelles de Fromage.

4 oz. [1 cup] Gruyère cheese, grated

Sift the flour and salt into a medium-sized mixing bowl. Make a well in the centre of the flour mixture and break the eggs into it. Add 1 tablespoon of the cream and stir the eggs and cream together with a wooden spoon, mixing well. Slowly incorporate the flour.

Add the remaining cream, a little at a time. Continue mixing until all the flour and half the cream is blended to make a thick batter. With a wire whisk or rotary beater, beat in the rest of the cream and 1 tablespoon of the oil. Continue beating until the batter is smooth. Stir in the cheese. Cover and set aside for 30 minutes.

With a pastry brush, grease a medium-sized, heavy frying-pan with a little of the remaining oil. Place the pan over moderate heat and heat the pan for 30 seconds or until it is very hot. Drop spoonfuls of the batter into the hot pan, well spaced. Cook for 2 minutes or until the pancakes are brown on the underside. Turn them over and brown the other sides. Transfer the pancakes to a warmed serving plate and keep them warm while you make the rest of the pancakes in the same way, adding more oil when necessary. Serve piping hot.

Quenelles de Fromage

CHEESE QUENELLES

These little crusty-topped Quenelles de Fromage have soft, melting centres. Serve them with creamed spinach garnished with croûtons as a light luncheon dish, or on their own as part of a hot buffet. A well-chilled white wine, such as Meursault or Pouilly Fuissé, would complement this dish nicely.

4 SERVINGS

6 oz. Brie or Camembert cheese
2 egg yolks
1 oz. [⅓ cup] fresh white breadcrumbs
1 teaspoon flour
½ teaspoon black pepper
2 tablespoons double [heavy] cream
2 tablespoons milk
1 teaspoon salt
1 tablespoon grated Parmesan cheese

In a medium-sized mixing bowl, mash the Brie or Camembert and the egg yolks together with a kitchen fork until they form a fairly smooth paste. Rub the cheese mixture through a fine wire strainer into another medium-sized mixing bowl. Discard any pulp remaining in the strainer. Stir the fresh breadcrumbs, reserving 1 tablespoon, the flour, black pepper, cream and milk into the cheese mixture.

Cover the bowl with a clean cloth and chill the mixture in the refrigerator for 30 minutes.

Preheat the oven to hot 425°F (Gas Mark 7, 220°C).

Half-fill a large saucepan with water and add the salt. Place the pan over moderately high heat and bring the water to the boil.

Remove the bowl from the refrigerator. Cut the cheese mixture into approximately 2- by 1-inch pieces and roll the pieces, between the hands, to form small sausage shapes.

Drop the sausage shapes into the boiling water, a few at a time. Cook for 30 seconds. As the quenelles rise to the surface, remove them from the pan with a slotted spoon and place them on a plate. Set aside and keep warm while the remaining shapes are cooked in the same way.

Arrange the quenelles in a shallow ovenproof dish.

In a small bowl, mix together the reserved breadcrumbs and the Parmesan cheese. Sprinkle the breadcrumb mixture over the quenelles and place the dish in the centre of the oven. Bake the quenelles for 10 minutes or until the cheese mixture has melted and become golden brown.

Remove the dish from the oven and serve the quenelles immediately, straight from the dish.

Four Cheeses with Italian Rice

☆ ① ① ✗

This delicious snack dish may be prepared in advance and chilled until it is baked.

4-6 SERVINGS

12 oz. [4⅔ cups] cooked Italian rice, such as avorio
1 small onion, finely chopped
1 celery stalk, trimmed and finely chopped
2 oz. [½ cup] Provolone cheese, grated
1½ oz. Bel Paese cheese, thinly sliced
3 oz. Fontina cheese, thinly sliced
3 oz. prosciutto, chopped
3 oz. [¾ cup] Parmesan cheese, finely grated
1½ oz. [3 tablespoons] butter, cut into small pieces

Preheat the oven to fairly hot 375°F (Gas Mark 5, 190°C).

Arrange one-quarter of the rice on the bottom of a large ovenproof dish. Sprinkle over one-third of the onion and celery. Cover with one-third of the Provolone, Bel Paese and Fontina. Cover with one-third of the prosciutto and one-quarter of the Parmesan cheese. Continue making layers in this way until all the ingredients are used up, ending with a layer of rice covered with Parmesan cheese.

Dot the butter pieces on top of the mixture and place the dish in a baking tin half-filled with boiling water.

Place the tin in the oven and bake for 30 minutes or until the top is bubbling.

Remove the tin from the oven and the dish from the tin. Serve immediately.

Roquefort and Cream Cheese Ring

☆ ☆ ① ① ① ✗ ✗

Roquefort and Cream Cheese Ring makes an impressive centrepiece for a summer buffet party.

6-8 SERVINGS

2 teaspoons vegetable oil
6 oz. Roquefort cheese, crumbled
8 oz. cream cheese
¼ teaspoon cayenne pepper
1 teaspoon anchovy essence
2 tablespoons finely chopped spring onions [scallions], green part only
½ oz. gelatine dissolved in 2 fl. oz. [¼ cup] hot water
6 fl. oz. [¾ cup] mayonnaise
6 fl. oz. double cream [¾ cup heavy cream]
8 lettuce leaves
12 tomato slices
8 stuffed olives, halved

With the 2 teaspoons of oil, grease a 1½-pint [1-quart] ring mould. Place the mould, upside-down, on kitchen paper towels to drain.

Using the back of a wooden spoon, rub the cheese through a fine strainer into a medium-sized mixing bowl. Beat in the cream cheese, cayenne, anchovy essence and spring onions [scallions].

Quickly stir the dissolved gelatine into the cheese mixture and continue stirring until all the ingredients are blended.

With a metal spoon, fold the mayonnaise and cream into the mixture. Pour the mixture into the ring mould. Place the mould in the refrigerator and leave to chill for 1 hour or until the mould has set.

Remove the ring mould from the refrigerator and quickly dip the bottom into hot water. Invert a serving plate over the mould, reverse the two and turn the cheese ring out on to the plate. The ring should slide out easily.

Garnish the ring with the lettuce leaves, tomato slices and halved olives. Serve immediately, or chill in the refrigerator until required.

Roquefort Mousse

☆ ☆ ① ① ① ✗ ✗ ✗

Serve Roquefort Mousse on toast or crusty bread as a first course for a special dinner.

4-6 SERVINGS

2 teaspoons vegetable oil
1 lb. Roquefort cheese, crumbled
8 fl. oz. single cream [1 cup light cream]
½ teaspoon ground cinnamon
12 fl. oz. double cream [1½ cups heavy cream], beaten until thick
½ oz. gelatine dissolved in 4 tablespoons hot water
small bunch mustard and cress, washed and shaken dry

With the oil, grease dariole moulds or individual dishes. Place them, upside-down, on kitchen paper towels to drain.

With the back of a wooden spoon, rub the cheese through a fine strainer into a large heatproof mixing bowl. Gradually pour the single [light] cream on to the cheese, beating constantly. Place the bowl over a saucepan half-filled with hot water. Add the cinnamon and stir constantly until the mixture becomes smooth.

Remove the pan from the heat and the bowl from the pan and allow to cool for 10 minutes. Place the bowl in the refrigerator and chill for 1 hour.

Remove the bowl from the refrigerator. Fold in the double [heavy] cream and the dissolved gelatine. Spoon the cheese mixture into the moulds or dishes and

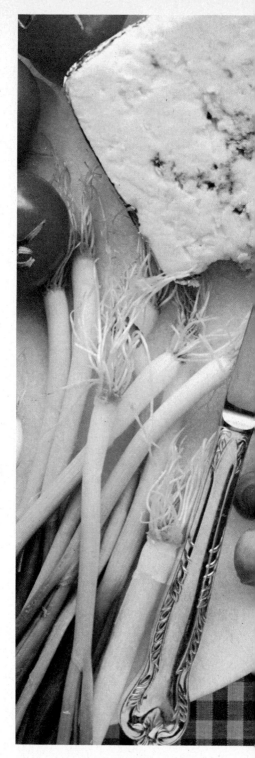

place in the refrigerator to chill for 1 hour or until the mousse is firm.

Remove the moulds or dishes from the refrigerator and run a knife around the edge of each one. Turn the mousse out on to individual plates and garnish with the mustard and cress. Serve immediately.

Sage and Cheese Bake

☆ ① ✗ ✗

A tasty dish to serve for a snack lunch or supper, Sage and Cheese Bake may be served with grilled [broiled] tomatoes.

4 SERVINGS

1 teaspoon butter
16 fl. oz. [2 cups] milk
8 oz. [2 cups] Cheddar cheese, finely
   grated
6 oz. [3 cups] fresh white
   breadcrumbs
2 teaspoons dried sage
½ small onion, finely chopped
½ teaspoon salt
¼ teaspoon black pepper
4 eggs, separated

Preheat the oven to moderate 350°F (Gas
Mark 4, 180°C). Using the butter, grease

a medium-sized ovenproof dish.

Pour the milk into a small saucepan set
over moderate heat. Scald the milk.
Remove the pan from the heat and set
the milk aside to cool to lukewarm.

In a large mixing bowl, combine the
cheese, breadcrumbs, sage, onion, salt,
pepper and egg yolks.

Gradually stir in the milk. Set the
breadcrumb mixture aside for 30 minutes
to soak.

In a large mixing bowl, beat the egg
whites with a wire whisk or rotary beater
until they form stiff peaks. Using a large
metal spoon, carefully fold the egg whites

*This glorious Roquefort and Cream
Cheese Ring makes the ideal centrepiece for a summer buffet. Serve
with well-chilled white wine and thin
slivers of toast.*

into the cheese mixture. Spoon the mixture into the prepared dish. Place the dish
in the oven and bake for 50 to 55 minutes
or until the top is golden brown and firmly
set.

Remove the dish from the oven and
serve the bake at once, straight from the
dish.

Shrimp and Cheese Mould

☆ ☆ ① ① ① ✕ ✕

Shrimp and Cheese Mould makes an appetizing first course for any dinner party, served with brown bread.

8-10 SERVINGS

1 teaspoon vegetable oil
½ cucumber, peeled and diced
1 tablespoon salt
3 tablespoons white wine vinegar
12 oz. cream cheese
4 fl. oz. double cream [½ cup heavy cream]
6 fl. oz. [¾ cup] mayonnaise
1 tablespoon paprika
½ teaspoon black pepper
2 tablespoons chopped fresh chives
½ oz. gelatine, dissolved in 2 fl. oz. [¼ cup] hot water
8 oz. frozen peeled shrimps, thawed and drained
1 bunch watercress, washed and shaken dry
5 tomatoes, quartered
9 black olives, stoned

With the teaspoon of oil, grease a 1½-pint [1-quart] ring mould. Place upside-down on kitchen paper towels and drain.

Place the cucumber in a colander and sprinkle over the salt and vinegar. Set aside for 1 hour to dégorge. Drain off any liquid and set aside.

In a medium-sized mixing bowl, beat the cheese with a wooden spoon until it is soft and creamy. Fold in the cream and mayonnaise. Stir in the paprika, pepper and chives. Add the dissolved gelatine mixture and continue stirring until all the ingredients are thoroughly blended.

Fold in the shrimps and cucumber. Pour the mixture into the prepared mould and place in the refrigerator. Chill for 1 hour or until the filling has set. Remove the mould from the refrigerator and quickly dip the bottom into hot water. Invert a serving dish over the mould and reverse the two, giving the mould a sharp shake. The mixture should slide out easily.

Garnish the ring with the watercress, tomato quarters and olives and serve.

Stilton Pâté

☆ ① ① ✕ ✕

A creamy, sharp-tasting pâté, adapted from an old English recipe, Stilton Pâté is an unusual first course. Serve with toast.

8-10 SERVINGS

24 fl. oz. [3 cups] milk

Rich and creamy Stilton Pâté – serve it with hot buttered toast.

1 large onion, coarsely chopped
1 carrot, scraped and chopped
2 celery stalks, chopped
  bouquet garni, consisting of 4 parsley sprigs, 1 thyme spray and 1 bay leaf tied together
3 oz. [⅜ cup] butter
3 oz. [¾ cup] flour
3 tablespoons mayonnaise
2 teaspoons lemon juice
3 garlic cloves, crushed
10 stuffed olives, finely chopped
½ teaspoon salt
½ teaspoon black pepper
⅛ teaspoon cayenne pepper
12 oz. Stilton cheese, rind removed, and crumbled

Pour the milk into a saucepan set over high heat. Bring the milk to the boil. Reduce the heat to low and add the onion, carrot, celery and bouquet garni. Cover and simmer for 15 minutes.

Remove the pan from the heat. Set the milk aside until it has cooled to room temperature. Pour the milk through a strainer into a large bowl, pressing on the vegetables with the back of a spoon to extract any juices. Discard the contents of the strainer and set the milk aside.

In a medium-sized saucepan, melt the butter over moderate heat. When the foam subsides, remove the pan from the heat and, using a wooden spoon, stir in the flour to make a smooth paste. Gradually add the milk, stirring constantly. Return the pan to the heat and cook, stirring constantly, for 2 to 3 minutes or until the sauce is very thick and smooth. Remove from the heat and set the sauce aside to cool to room temperature.

When the sauce is cool, beat in the mayonnaise, lemon juice, garlic and olives and season with the salt, pepper and cayenne. Place the cheese in a strainer set over a bowl. Using the back of a wooden spoon, rub the cheese through the strainer. Beat the cheese into the sauce until the mixture is smooth.

Spoon the mixture into a serving dish and smooth the surface with the back of the spoon. Place the pâté in the refrigerator to chill for 1 hour. Serve.

Tomato-Filled Cheese Choux Pastry Ring

☆ ☆ ① ① ✕

Tomato-Filled Cheese Choux Pastry Ring is an adaptation of the classic French gougère. Serve with a green salad.

6 SERVINGS

1 oz. [2 tablespoons] plus 1 teaspoon butter
1 medium-sized onion, thinly sliced

1 oz. [¼ cup] flour
4 fl. oz. [½ cup] chicken stock
3 tablespoons tomato chutney
3 large tomatoes, blanched, peeled and chopped
4 oz. prawns or shrimps, shelled
¼ teaspoon salt
¼ teaspoon black pepper
2 oz. [½ cup] Cheddar cheese, grated

PASTRY

5 fl. oz. [⅝ cup] water
1½ oz. [3 tablespoons] butter, cut into small pieces
½ teaspoon salt
¼ teaspoon cayenne pepper
¼ teaspoon dry mustard
5 oz. [1¼ cups] flour
2 large eggs
1 egg white
2 oz. [½ cup] Cheddar cheese, grated
¼ teaspoon black pepper

Using the teaspoon of butter, grease a 12-inch ovenproof flan dish.

First make the pastry. In a saucepan, bring the water to the boil over moderate heat. Add the butter, salt, cayenne and mustard. When the butter has melted, remove the pan from the heat and beat in the flour. Beat until the mixture pulls away from the sides of the pan.

Beat the eggs and the egg white into the mixture, beating each one until it is blended before adding the next. When the eggs and the egg white have been absorbed, the mixture should be thick and smooth. Stir in the cheese and pepper.

Preheat the oven to fairly hot 400°F (Gas Mark 6, 200°C).

In a large saucepan, melt the remaining butter over moderate heat. When the foam subsides, add the onion to the pan and cook, stirring occasionally, for 5 to 7 minutes or until the onion is soft and translucent but not brown. Remove the pan from the heat and, with a wooden spoon, stir in the flour to make a smooth paste. Gradually add the stock, stirring constantly. Return the pan to the heat and cook, stirring constantly, for 2 to 3 minutes or until the sauce is thick and smooth. Remove the pan from the heat and stir in the chutney, tomatoes, prawns or shrimps, salt and pepper.

Spoon the reserved dough mixture in large mounds, ½-inch apart, around the edge of the flan dish. Using another large spoon, spoon the tomato and prawn or shrimp mixture into the centre. Sprinkle the grated cheese over the top and place the dish in the oven. Cook for 30 to 35 minutes or until the pastry has doubled in size and is light brown in colour.

Remove the dish from the oven and pierce the pastry with a knife to allow the steam to escape. Serve immediately.

Brie Cheese Croquettes

☆ ① ① ✗

These delicious Brie Cheese Croquettes may be served with drinks.

25 CROQUETTES

10 oz. Brie cheese, rind removed
1½ oz. [3 tablespoons] butter
6 tablespoons flour
10 fl. oz. [1¼ cups] milk
¼ teaspoon white pepper
¼ teaspoon cayenne pepper
1 egg yolk
1 egg, lightly beaten
2 oz. [⅔ cup] dry breadcrumbs
   sufficient vegetable oil for
   deep-frying

With a wooden spoon, press the cheese through a strainer and set aside.

In a medium-sized saucepan, melt the butter over moderate heat. Remove the pan from the heat and stir in the flour to make a smooth paste. Gradually add the milk, stirring constantly. Return the pan to the heat and cook, stirring constantly, for 2 to 3 minutes or until the sauce is thick and smooth. Remove the pan from the heat and stir in the pepper and cayenne. Allow the mixture to cool.

When the mixture is lukewarm, stir in the egg yolk and strained cheese. Turn the mixture on to a plate and place it in the refrigerator to chill.

Remove the mixture from the refrigerator and, with floured hands, shape the mixture into walnut-sized balls. Dip the balls in the beaten egg, then roll them in the breadcrumbs.

Fill a deep-frying pan one-third full with vegetable oil. Place the pan over moderate heat and heat the oil until it registers 350°F on a deep-fat thermometer or until a small cube of stale bread dropped into the oil becomes golden in 55 seconds. Carefully lower the croquettes, a few at a time, into the oil. Cook for 1 minute or until they are crisp and golden.

Remove the croquettes from the oil and drain on kitchen paper towels. Serve.

Creamed Camembert

☆ ① ① ✗ ✗ ✗

A superb cheese-wine spread, Creamed Camembert is delicious on cocktail biscuits as an hors d'oeuvre.

4 SERVINGS

5 oz. Camembert cheese
2 fl. oz. [¼ cup] dry white wine
2 oz. [¼ cup] unsalted butter,
   softened

With a small, sharp knife, cut the rind off

These spicy, crisp little Brie Cheese Croquettes are a mixture of cheese, breadcrumbs, milk and cayenne pepper. Serve as an unusual appetizer with cocktails.

the cheese and discard it. Put the cheese in a china bowl. Spread the cheese out so that it covers the bottom of the bowl. Pour over the wine to cover the cheese. Cover the bowl and leave, at room temperature, for at least 12 hours.

Drain off any excess wine and, using a wooden spoon, beat in the butter until the mixture is a smooth, creamy paste.

With your hands, reshape the cheese mixture into a round and allow it to harden a little. Do not chill it.

Cheese and Chive Spread

☆ ① ✗

This quick and easy-to-make cream cheese spread is delicious served in baked potatoes or sandwiches, or as an accompaniment to charcoal grilled [broiled] steak. It may also be served as a cocktail party dip with celery stalks and carrot sticks.

ABOUT 8 OUNCE [1 CUP] SPREAD

8 oz. cream cheese
3 tablespoons finely chopped fresh
   chives
2 tablespoons single [light] cream
⅛ teaspoon salt
¼ teaspoon black pepper
⅛ teaspoon cayenne pepper

Combine all the ingredients together in a medium-sized mixing bowl, and using a wooden spoon, mix them to a soft cream.

Chill slightly before serving.

Creamy Cheese Dip

☆ ① ① ✗

Quick and easy to prepare, this Creamy Cheese Dip is ideal to serve with crudités for a party or buffet.

2 POUNDS

16 oz. cottage cheese
8 fl. oz. [1 cup] sour cream
5 oz. Roquefort cheese
8 spring onions [scallions], chopped
4 tablespoons mayonnaise
½ teaspoon salt
1 teaspoon black pepper

In a large bowl, mix the cottage cheese and sour cream together with a wooden spoon until the mixture is creamy. Put the Roquefort cheese in a small bowl and mash it well with a fork.

Mix the Roquefort into the cream cheese mixture and stir well.

Stir in the spring onions [scallions], mayonnaise, salt and pepper. Taste and add more salt and pepper if necessary. Chill in the refrigerator before serving.

Gorgonzola Biscuits

☆ ① ① ✗ ✗

Flavourful savoury biscuits which use a fine Italian cheese, these Gorgonzola Biscuits may be served on their own with drinks or after the main course of a meal with cheese.

40 BISCUITS

2 oz. [¼ cup] butter
6 oz. Gorgonzola cheese
8 oz. [2 cups] flour, sifted
1 egg
¼ teaspoon salt
¼ teaspoon black pepper

1 tablespoon water (optional)

In a medium-sized mixing bowl, cream the butter with a wooden spoon until it is soft. Add the cheese and mash it into the butter. Cream well. Blend in the flour, egg, salt and pepper. Knead the mixture lightly to form a smooth dough. If the dough is too dry, add the water. Cover the dough and place it in the refrigerator to chill for 30 minutes.

Preheat the oven to hot 425°F (Gas Mark 7, 220°C).

On a lightly floured surface, roll out the dough into a rectangular shape ¼-inch thick. Trim the edges of the dough and cut into 1-inch squares with a sharp knife. Transfer the squares to a large baking sheet and place it in the oven. Bake the biscuits for 12 to 15 minutes or until they are golden brown.

Remove the baking sheet from the oven and cool the biscuits on a wire rack.

These delicious savoury Gorgonzola Biscuits may be served as a strongly-flavoured snack with drinks.

Cheese and Spinach Canapés

☆ ① ⧗

An unusual and tempting mixture of spinach and cheese on crisp croûtes, Cheese and Spinach Canapés may be served with cocktails. The canapés may be prepared well in advance and reheated by grilling [broiling], just before serving.

24 CANAPES

  1 teaspoon salt
1½ lb. spinach, washed and
    stalks removed
  2 oz. [¼ cup] butter
  ½ teaspoon freshly ground
    black pepper
  3 oz. [¾ cup] Cheddar cheese,
    grated
  1 tablespoon olive oil
24 triangles of white bread
  1 oz. [⅓ cup] fine dry white
    breadcrumbs
  1 oz. [2 tablespoons] butter, melted

Half-fill a large saucepan with cold water. Add the salt and bring the water to the boil over high heat. Put the spinach in the pan and reduce the heat to moderate.

Cook the spinach for 7 to 12 minutes or until it is tender.

Drain the spinach in a colander and squeeze it dry between two plates. Chop it finely and return it to the saucepan. Add 1 ounce [2 tablespoons] of the butter, the pepper and two-thirds of the cheese and stir to mix. Cover the pan and set it aside in a warm place.

In a large frying-pan, melt the remaining butter with the oil over moderately high heat. When the foam subsides, add the triangles of bread.

Fry for 10 minutes on each side, or until browned.

Remove the croûtes from the pan with a slotted spoon and place them on kitchen paper towels to drain.

Preheat the grill [broiler] to high.

Place a tablespoon of the spinach and cheese mixture on each croûte and top with the remaining cheese, breadcrumbs and melted butter.

Place the canapés under the grill [broiler] and cook for 2 to 3 minutes or until they are hot and the cheese lightly browned.

Serve at once.

Cheesecake

☆ ☆ ① ① ⧖

This popular sweet-sour confection probably originated in Greece and is now world famous. There are hundreds of variations, but the basic ingredients are similar, cottage, curd or cream cheese, eggs and a thickening such as flour, cornflour [corn-starch], semolina or ground nuts. Extra ingredients are added for flavour; fresh or dried fruits, essences and spices being the most usual. Cheesecake generally has a pastry or biscuit [cookie] crust as a base and some recipes require baking and others are just chilled in the refrigerator.

ONE 9-INCH CAKE

3 oz. [⅜ cup] plus 1 teaspoon butter, melted
6 oz. digestive biscuits [3 cups graham crackers], crushed
2 tablespoons sugar

FILLING

1½ lb. full fat cream cheese
3 oz. [⅜ cup] sugar
3 eggs, separated
1 teaspoon grated lemon rind
1 tablespoon cornflour [cornstarch] mixed with 2 tablespoons lemon juice
2 oz. [⅓ cup] currants
1½ oz. [¼ cup] glacé cherries, chopped
5 fl. oz. [⅝ cup] sour cream
2 teaspoons castor sugar
½ teaspoon vanilla essence

Preheat the oven to moderate 350°F (Gas Mark 4, 180°C).

With the teaspoon of butter, grease a 9-inch loose-bottomed cake tin.

In a medium-sized mixing bowl combine the crushed digestive biscuits [graham crackers], sugar and remaining butter with a wooden spoon. Spoon the mixture into the cake tin and press it firmly, covering the bottom of the tin.

This rich Cheesecake is guaranteed to have them coming back for more!

In a large mixing bowl, combine the cream cheese and sugar with a wooden spoon. Add the egg yolks and beat the mixture until it is smooth. Stir in the lemon rind, cornflour [cornstarch] mixture, currants and glacé cherries.

In another large mixing bowl, beat the egg whites with a wire whisk or rotary beater until they form stiff peaks. Fold the egg whites into the cheese mixture.

Spoon the mixture into the prepared tin. Bake in the centre of the oven for 20 minutes or until the centre is firm when pressed with a fingertip.

In a mixing bowl, combine the sour cream, castor sugar and vanilla essence.

Remove the tin from the oven and, using a palette knife, spread the sour cream mixture over the top of the cake. Return the cake to the oven and bake for a further 5 minutes.

Remove the tin from the oven and set aside to cool. When cool remove the cake from the tin and chill it in the refrigerator before serving.

Crostata di Ricotta

CHEESE PIE

☆ ☆ ① ① ① ✕ ✕ ✕

This rich, creamy cheese pie is one of the most famous of all Italian cheesecakes. If you are unable to buy ricotta, any whole-curd cottage cheese may be substituted.

ONE 9-INCH PIE

PASTRY

6 oz. [¾ cup] plus 1 teaspoon butter, cut into small pieces
8 oz. [2 cups] flour
¼ teaspoon salt
4 egg yolks, lightly beaten
2 tablespoons sugar
5 tablespoons Marsala
grated rind of 1 lemon

FILLING

2½ lb. ricotta cheese, strained
4 oz. [½ cup] sugar
2 tablespoons flour
¼ teaspoon salt
½ teaspoon vanilla essence
grated rind of 1 orange
grated rind and juice of 2 lemons
4 egg yolks
3 tablespoons raisins
2 tablespoons finely chopped candied peel
2 tablespoons slivered, blanched almonds
1 egg white, lightly beaten

Moist Crostata di Ricotta is Italian in origin and absolutely irresistable to taste.

With the teaspoon of butter, grease a 9-inch springform pan and set aside.

To make the pastry, sift the flour and salt into a large mixing bowl. Make a well in the centre of the flour and into it drop the remaining butter, the egg yolks, sugar, Marsala and lemon rind.

With your fingertips, combine all of the ingredients and lightly knead the dough until it is smooth and can be formed into a ball. Do not over handle it.

Cover the dough and refrigerate it for about 1 hour, or until it is fairly firm.

Break off about one-quarter of the dough. Dust it with flour, cover it and put it back in the refrigerator.

Reshape the rest of the dough into a ball. On a floured board, flatten the ball into a circle.

Sprinkle flour over the top of the dough circle and roll it out into a circle 2 inches wider in diameter than the springform pan.

Lift the dough on the rolling pin and lay it over the pan. Gently ease the dough into the pan.

With a knife, trim off the excess dough round the rim of the pan. Set the

dough case aside.

Preheat the oven to moderate 350°F (Gas Mark 4, 180°C).

In a medium-sized mixing bowl, beat the ricotta cheese, sugar, flour, salt, vanilla essence, grated orange and lemon rind, lemon juice and egg yolks together with a wooden spoon until they are well combined. Stir in the raisins and candied peel.

Spoon the mixture into the pastry case, spreading it out evenly with a spatula. Sprinkle the top with the almonds.

Remove the reserved dough from the refrigerator and roll it out into a rectangle, at least 10 inches long. With a sharp knife, cut the dough into long strips. Arrange the dough strips over the filling to make a lattice pattern.

Using a pastry brush, brush the strips with the beaten egg white.

Place the pie in the oven and bake for 1 hour, or until the crust is golden brown and the filling is firm to the touch.

Remove the pie from the oven and place it on a wire cake rack.

Carefully undo the spring and remove the outside rim of the pan. Leave the pie to cool.

When the pie is cool, carefully slide a knife between the crust and the pan bottom and slide the pie carefully on to a dish.

61

Coeur à la Crème

☆　　①　①　　✂　✂　✂

This is an attractive, light classic French dessert. Coeur à la Crème is traditionally served with wild strawberries and sprinkled with sugar.

6 SERVINGS

1 lb. cream cheese
⅛ teaspoon salt
10 fl. oz. double cream [1¼ cups heavy cream]
2 egg whites
2 tablespoons soft brown sugar

Gently rub the cream cheese and salt through a strainer into a large mixing bowl. Using a wooden spoon, beat in the cream until it is thoroughly blended and the mixture is smooth.

In a mixing bowl, beat the egg whites with a wire whisk or rotary beater until they form stiff peaks. With a metal spoon, fold them into the cheese mixture.

With a layer of cheesecloth, line 6 *coeur à la crème* moulds if you have them. If not, use 6 small moulds with perforated bottoms. Spoon the cheese mixture into the moulds.

Stand the moulds in a large soup dish or plate to catch the liquid that will drain out of the cheese mixture and put both the moulds and dish into the refrigerator

Coeur à la Crème, a classic French confection, is a mixture of cream cheese and cream with brown sugar.

for 12 hours or overnight.

Invert the moulds on to a serving platter and remove the cheesecloth lining. Place a teaspoon of brown sugar on top of each coeur à la crème and serve them accompanied by a jug of cream.

Cream Cheese Delight

☆　　①　①　①　✂　✂

This scrumptious mixture of mandarin oranges, cream, cream cheese and apple sauce may be served as an elegant end to a dinner party.

6 SERVINGS

8 oz. cream cheese
10 fl. oz. double cream [1¼ cups heavy cream]
4 fl. oz. [½ cup] thick apple sauce
2 tablespoons castor sugar
22 oz. canned mandarin oranges, drained and with the can juice reserved
1 teaspoon grated orange rind
2 tablespoons medium sherry juice of 1 lemon
½ oz. gelatine, dissolved in 4

tablespoons hot water
2 tablespoons slivered almonds, toasted

In a bowl, beat the cream cheese with a wooden spoon until it is soft and fluffy. Using a metal spoon, gradually fold the cream into the cheese so that they are thoroughly combined. Stir in the apple sauce, sugar and about three-quarters of the mandarin oranges. Set aside.

Pour the reserved can juice into a medium-sized mixing bowl and stir in the orange rind, sherry and lemon juice. Add the gelatine and beat well to blend.

Gradually pour the gelatine mixture into the cream mixture, beating constantly. When the ingredients are combined, pour the mixture into a large mould. Place the mould in the refrigerator to chill for 2 hours or until it is set.

Remove the mould from the refrigerator and dip the bottom quickly into hot water. Run a knife around the edge of the mould to loosen the mixture. Place a serving plate, inverted, over the mould and reverse the two, giving the mould a sharp shake. The mixture should slide out easily.

Arrange the remaining mandarin oranges decoratively over the top of the mixture and scatter over the toasted almonds. Serve at once.

Maids of Honour

☆ ① ① ⋈ ⋈

These little cakes originated in Richmond, Surrey. The story goes that when Henry VIII lived in Richmond Palace, he was inspecting the kitchens and saw someone trying a new recipe for cakes. He liked them so much that he asked the maid of honour to continue making the cakes.

Eventually, the secret recipe was given to a baker who had a shop in Richmond and so Maids of Honour cakes became famous. Although the old shop was destroyed, the recipe was passed on to another baker and this shop is now in Kew, Surrey.

12 CAKES

PASTRY
- 8 oz. [1 cup] plus 2 teaspoons unsalted butter
- 8 oz. [2 cups] flour
- ¼ teaspoon salt
- 5 fl. oz. [⅝ cup] iced water

FILLING
- 4 oz. [½ cup] curd cheese
- 4 oz. [½ cup] butter
- 4 oz. [½ cup] sugar
- 4 egg yolks
- 1 medium-sized potato, cooked and mashed
- 2 oz. [⅓ cup] ground almonds grated rind of 1 lemon
- ¼ teaspoon grated nutmeg
- 3 fl. oz. [⅜ cup] brandy

With the 2 teaspoons of butter, grease 12 patty tins. Set aside.

To make the pastry, sift the flour and salt into a medium-sized mixing bowl. With a knife, cut 2 ounces [¼ cup] of the butter into the flour.

With your fingertips, rub the butter into the flour until the mixture resembles fine breadcrumbs. Add the water and mix to a firm dough. Cover the dough with greaseproof or waxed paper and put it in the refrigerator to chill for 15 minutes.

Put the remaining butter between two pieces of greaseproof or waxed paper. Beat it with the back of a wooden spoon or mallet into a flat oblong about ¾-inch thick.

On a floured board, roll out the dough into a rectangular shape ¼-inch thick. Place the oblong of butter in the centre of the dough. Fold the dough over it to make a parcel. Cover the dough and put it in the refrigerator for 10 minutes.

Place the dough, with the folds downwards, on the board and roll it out away from you into a rectangle. Fold the rectangle in three. Turn so that the open end is facing you and roll out again. Cover the dough and put it in the refrigerator to chill for 15 minutes. Repeat this rolling and folding twice more.

Preheat the oven to fairly hot 400°F (Gas Mark 6, 200°C).

To prepare the filling, in a medium-sized mixing bowl, combine the cheese, butter and sugar with a wooden spoon.

In a small mixing bowl, beat the egg yolks with a wire whisk or rotary beater until they are thick and creamy. Pour the egg yolks into the cheese mixture and mix well. Add the potato, ground almonds, lemon rind, nutmeg and brandy. Stir well until all the ingredients are thoroughly mixed. Set the filling aside.

On a floured board, roll out the dough until it is about ¼-inch thick. With a 4-inch pastry cutter, cut the dough into twelve circles. Line the bottoms and sides of the prepared patty tins with the dough circles. Fill each dough case with a spoonful of the filling.

Place the patty tins on a baking sheet and put it in the oven. Bake for 20 to 25 minutes or until the pastry is golden.

Carefully remove the cakes from their tins and set aside on a wire rack to cool completely before serving.

Maids of Honour are little cheese cakes first popularized by Henry VIII.

Mexican Cheese Squares

☆ ① ⋈ ⋈

Pastry, filled with cottage cheese mixed with egg and fruit, then cut into little squares, Mexican Cheese Squares are delicious.

8 SQUARES

12 oz. [3 cups] flour
¼ teaspoon salt
6 oz. [¾ cup] butter, chilled
2 small eggs, lightly beaten
3 to 4 tablespoons iced water
2 tablespoons milk
FILLING
8 oz. cottage cheese, strained
1 egg, beaten with 2 egg yolks
4 oz. [½ cup] castor sugar
3 oz. [½ cup] currants
1 teaspoon lemon juice
¼ teaspoon vanilla essence

Sift the flour and salt into a large mixing bowl. Add the butter and cut it into small pieces with a table knife. With your fingertips, rub the butter into the flour until the mixture resembles breadcrumbs.

Add the eggs with 2 tablespoons of the water and mix into the flour with the knife.

Knead the dough gently and form it into a ball. Chill in the refrigerator for 30 minutes.

Preheat the oven to fairly hot 400°F (Gas Mark 6, 200°C).

To make the filling, place all the ingredients in a bowl and beat together until they are mixed.

Remove the dough from the refrigerator and divide it in half. On a lightly floured board, roll out half of the dough to a rectangle large enough to line a 7- x 11-inch baking sheet. Lift the dough on to the rolling pin and place it on the baking sheet. Spoon the filling on to the dough, spreading it out evenly to within ¼-inch of the edges. Moisten the edges of the dough with a little water.

Roll the remaining dough out to a rectangle large enough to cover the filling. Lift the dough on to the filling, pressing the edges together to seal. Cut a slit in the centre of the dough and trim the edges. Brush the top of the dough with the milk.

Place the baking sheet in the oven and bake the dough for 20 to 25 minutes or until it is golden brown.

Remove the sheet from the oven and set it aside to cool. Cut the pastry into 8 squares and serve.

Cheese Strudel

☆ ☆ ① ⋈ ⋈

Cheese Strudel takes a long time to make, but the finished dish is delicious.

6-8 SERVINGS

10 oz. [2½ cups] flour
½ teaspoon salt
1 egg, lightly beaten
7 fl. oz. [⅞ cup] tepid water
1 oz. [2 tablespoons] butter, melted
FILLING
1½ lb. cottage cheese
2 oz. [¼ cup] sugar
2 eggs, lightly beaten
¼ teaspoon salt
  grated rind of 1 lemon
4 oz. [⅔ cup] sultanas or raisins
4 oz. [½ cup] butter, melted
2 oz. [1 cup] fresh breadcrumbs

Sift the flour and salt into a large bowl. Beat the egg, water and butter together until they are well blended. Stir the egg and water mixture into the flour and mix well. Knead with your hands until a firm dough is formed.

Place the dough on a floured board and continue kneading for about 10 minutes until it is smooth and elastic. Place the dough in a warmed, large mixing bowl. Cover the bowl and set it in a warm, draught-free place for 30 minutes.

Meanwhile, prepare the filling. In a bowl, combine the cheese, sugar, eggs, salt, lemon rind and sultanas or raisins, beating until they are well blended.

Spread out a large, clean cloth on a table. Sprinkle with flour. Place the dough on the cloth and roll out the dough as thinly as possible.

Lift and stretch the dough, pulling the dough until it is paper thin. This should be done as carefully as possible. Do not worry if a few small holes appear. With scissors, trim the outer edges of the dough so that the sides are straight.

Preheat the oven to very hot 450°F (Gas Mark 8, 230°C). Grease two baking sheets with half the melted butter.

Brush the dough with half the remaining melted butter and sprinkle with nearly all the breadcrumbs. Spoon the cheese in a long strip on to the dough, 3 inches away from the edges of the sides.

Using the cloth, lift the dough over the filling and roll it up Swiss [jelly] roll style. Tuck in the ends. Brush the top with the remaining melted butter and cover with the rest of the breadcrumbs.

With a sharp knife, divide the strudel into pieces long enough to fit the baking sheets. Place the strudels on the baking sheets with the seams underneath. Put the baking sheets in the oven and bake for 10 minutes. Reduce the oven temperature to fairly hot 400°F (Gas Mark 6, 200°C) and bake for a further 20 minutes, or until the strudels are golden brown.